IT'S TIME TO REMEMBER:

A Riveting Story of One Woman's

Awakening

to Alien Beings

by

Joy S. Gilbert

IT'S TIME TO REMEMBER

A Riveting Story of One Woman's Awakening to Alien Beings
by Joy S. Gilbert

Published by:

Laughing Bear Publishing
P.O. Box 40788
Eugene, Oregon 97404
U.S.A.

FIRST EDITION
1st Printing

Library of Congress
Catalog Card Number: 95-094261

ISBN # 0-9645941-4-5

PRINTED IN THE UNITED STATES
OF AMERICA
10 9 8 7 6 5 4 3 2

DEDICATION

To you in your peaceful brilliance we call to.

The song you've heard in the wind,

The sound in the silence, is where we touch your heart.

It is for you we come.

It is your welfare we care for.

It is your peace we seek.

We are here with you in your dream,

And in the woven fibers of your sleep.

friends
Joy S. Gilbert

TABLE OF CONTENTS

ACKNOWLEDGMENT

This book is written in appreciation of my *friends,* the custodians and guardians of the world I now embrace.
I thank my daughter, who wishes to remain unnamed, for the gifts that she has given me. Her unending need for appropriate guidance and truth compelled me to pursue the wisdom, deep within myself. It is the unconditional love I feel as a mother that expands my heart.
I thank my husband, Mark, who believed I could accomplish anything. While not always understanding my views on life, he respected my right to be who I am. His love provided me the support, the space, and the time to complete this work.
Peggy Snicale was the first person I told about my *Alien Abduction.* She pointed me in the right direction, enabling me to deal with my initial shock. I will always be deeply grateful to her.
Maggie Matoba was always there, woven into the fabric, unfolding before me. She provided me an open receptacle, to spill into, all the beauty my *friends* unveiled. Maggie asked me the questions that unleashed a thousand memories. I cherish her presence in my life.
I also want to thank George Karabinis, Maggie's husband. His kind and sweet nature longs for truth. He sanctioned the possibility of my *friends* and other realities.
Connie and Brian King not only *believed* in my relationship to these precious beings, but helped sustain me during my transition. Their friendship has brought a special

closeness with them to my whole family. My dear friend Ruth Adams believed in me when logic told her not to. Her heart sought to help me see my visions more clearly. Ruth's extraordinary nature and expansive awareness fills me with a deep love for her. I appreciate her contributions to my life. Ruth's husband, Chuck has been incredibly kind. Underlying each exchange that took place between us was his open mind and warm feelings. Although unspoken, I felt genuine love and support from him.

I cherish Rita Waleri who listened to my ramblings. She not only showed an interest in my work, but encouraged me. During the time we shared, Rita made valuable comments on my work. She is always there with a kind word and the knowledge of *what* it is that connects us.

There will always be a place in my heart for Bettye Hagan, whose bright and open eyes reveal her depth. Her thoughts stem from a place of knowing. Living in the knowledge of her own perfection, her powerful, yet sweet spirit flows out in loving kindness, fulfilling creation. I deeply treasure and love her.

I thank Catherine Harris, owner of Peralandra Books and Music for her enlightened contribution to the Eugene area. With taste and integrity, she established a business that feeds and nurtures the inner needs of our community, promoting books and music that stimulate awareness and spiritual growth. Her store provided me the books I needed after my *Alien Abduction.*

I deeply appreciate the time and information that Donald MacGregor, Ph.D. selflessly provided. Without a fee he offered me his knowledge of the *Alien Abduction* phenomenon. He allowed me the room to express myself and a place to release my waning feelings of insanity. I thank Linda and Robert Ackerman for their everpresent friendship. Together their deep love for one another emanates out into the atmosphere, serving creation in a powerfully, exalted manner. They kindly took the time from their busy schedules to read my manuscript and offer me their perceptions.

In the summer of 1993 I contacted the Bigelow Foundation in an effort to connect with others who had similar experiences. It was at this time that I had the pleasure of meeting Angela Thompson. Instantly, I felt a strong rapport with her. Through her kindness and willingness to provide me with information, I was able to connect with others who had similar experiences. Angela provided me the knowledge that these encounters occurred to credible, respected citizens. I deeply appreciate her contributions to my *realization.*

I thank Peter Anthony of Anthony Design in Eugene, Oregon, for his support. He set-up the graphic design for the dust cover and provided me with needed publishing information. I deeply appreciate his knowledge.

Charlie Magee of Signal Design in Eugene, Oregon, illustrated the dust jacket. He spent hours manipulating my photograph with colors and different hues to come up with the perfect cover. I appreciate his talent and his artistic sense.

I want to thank Camille Cole. She assisted me by not only placing my commas in the right place, but by sharing her knowledge of writing. Camille helped me write what I truly *felt.*

I deeply appreciate the love and support that Helen and Bill Shela, my parents, have provided me throughout the years. In their hearts they were the best parents they could be. They wanted me to have all the good things life had to offer. Nourishing my curiosity, they allowed me to find my own way in the world, never stifling my need to explore.

Last I want to express my deep love for my sister, Lynnie, who goes by the name of Elizabeth Heck. Over the years we have worked through sibling rivalry and trivial family feuds. She and I have come to know the truth about each other. There is a love between our spirits that is deeply connected to our souls. My heart is greatly enhanced by her presence in my life.

Penguin USA, permitted the use of Luigi Parandello's quote, translated by Edward Storer, *Three Plays: Six Characters in Search of an Author.*

FOREWORD

According to three Roper Organization polls, it has been estimated that around 2% of the American population (1 out of every 50, or approximately 5 million, adult Americans) may have had UFO abduction experiences. Abductees claim a "constellation of experiences" including: waking up paralyzed with a sense of a strange person or presence or something else in the room: seeing, either as a child or as an adult, a terrifying figure, in the bedroom, closet or elsewhere; feeling as if they had left their body; experiencing a period of missing time of an hour or more in which the person was apparently lost, but could not remember why or where they had been; seeing a ghost; feeling that they were actually flying through the air although they didn't know how or why; seeing an unusual light or balls of light in a room without knowing what was causing them, or where they came from; finding puzzling scars on their body that neither they nor anybody else could remember how or where they were received; seeing a UFO; and having vivid dreams about UFOs.

These are the kinds of experiences that Joy Gilbert writes about. Documenting her own experiences, she recounts her initial sightings and dreams, and her subsequent remembering of an ongoing interaction with non-human beings whom she calls her friends, which simultaneously terrifies and astonishes her.

Unable to place her experiences within the context of accepted reality, she gets on with her life. However, the interfaces are pervasive and she is forced to face the challenge of uncovering what they are and what they mean to her. She begins to remember. Joy discovers who her secret friends are and how they have influenced and guided her life, a life filled with wonder and joy and learning. Finally, she is able to directly communicate with her friends and uses their words to write the final chapter of her book.

Critics would like to write Joy off as either delusional or a crank but she is neither. She is an intelligent, educated and spiritual woman who has had her share of tough times and has prevailed with her mental health intact. Unlike many abductees, Joy sees her experiences as transformative and her view is currently recognized by many people who have integrated similar experiences.

Over the spectrum of human population, people will react differently to the same situation and this will color their interpretation of their experiences. A small percentage will react poorly to whatever life throws at them. Others will cope well. Initially, the first abductees seen by researchers Budd Hopkins and David Jacobs were individuals who were traumatized by their experiences, leading them to interpret abduction experiences as "bad." I share Joy's caution in labeling the interfacers as "good" or "bad." We cannot judge them by human values and morals. -- They are not human. Until we know their motives we cannot label their actions. Perhaps Joy's courageous recounting of her experiences will help us to understand their reasons for choosing to interact with us.

Angela Thompson, MS.
Former Research Coordinator of the Bigelow Foundation
February 1995

PREFACE

*"We must learn to reawaken and keep
ourselves awake, not by mechanical aids,
but by an infinite expectation of the dawn,
which does not forsake us in our soundest
sleep. I know of no more encouraging fact
than the unquestionable ability of man to
elevate his life by a conscious endeavor. It
is something to be able to paint a particular
picture, or to carve a statue, and so to make
a few objects beautiful; but it is far more
glorious to carve and paint the very
atmosphere and medium through which we
look, which morally we can do, to affect the
quality of the day, which is the highest of
arts."*

-Henry David Thoreau

Steven Spielberg's movies *ET* and *Close Encounters of
a Third Kind,* were my only prelude to the UFO
phenomenon. From time to time I caught news flashes
about sightings and heard the lurid descriptions of
abductee's sexual assaults. But any truth to these
allegations, I believed, were lost to their sensational nature.
I knew *something* was happening. But I didn't think the

media was getting the facts. And since it had nothing to do with me, I paid no attention.

Scanning the channels on TV one evening in the early eighties, I briefly paused when I saw a man in disguise, sharing his account of an *Alien Abduction*. Chilling and compelling, his narrative aroused profound feelings in me. The intensity of his emotions forced me to acknowledge that *something* had really happened. Unable to move, I paused on that station, thinking, "Thank God, nothing like that has ever happened to me." I advanced the channel.

Like many, I had conceded we weren't the only intelligent life in the universe. Nevertheless, it was impossible for me to believe that intelligent life manifested in spaceships; particularly ones that looked like they came right out of a science fiction film. For me, they didn't exist. However, from my earliest memory I experienced the feeling of being protected and guided by unseen forces.

Magical notions like Santa Claus, were real for me. In Sunday school I loved the stories about Jesus and took their principles to heart. I believed in angels and miracles. Often, after my family went to sleep at night, I spent hours searching the night sky. Not really understanding why, I looked to the stars for answers. Wondering what I was doing here, I felt I'd forgotten *something*. And that *something*, was urgently awaiting my *remembering*.

Sometimes at night, when the house was still, a man would appear in my room. Wearing a double breasted trench coat, cinched at the waist and a 1940's fedora hat, he stood a few feet from my bed. He would watch me as I lay in that place between wakefulness and sleep. Easily I shared my secret thoughts and dreams with him. Never really seeing his face, I believed he was my grandfather. Together, we'd journey to a tranquil lush green meadow with gently rolling hills. Flourishing with tall, softly waving grass, its silent splendor was broken only by a medley of brilliant flowers. In a flash, a towering willow would appear. Engulfed in a swirling luminous blue-white light, my night-time friend and I would find ourselves spellbound under its awesome swaying boughs. I was in heaven.

In later years, the sweetness of those memories sustained me when life seemed filled with more pain than I could bear. It is only now I have realized that those apparitions were related to the UFO phenomenon.

My grandfather, a retired attorney and judge, died when I was three. My memories of him were fixed on the time he spent caring for his garden. He always wore a funny looking hat. Pulling it down over his forehead, he would shade his failing eyes from the brightness of the sun. When the image of a man wearing a fedora hat appeared in my room, I assumed it was my grandfather. Kind, loving, and gentle, my grandfather always made me feel special, loved. So did the man who appeared in my room.

I knew my grandfather was dead. Yet the feeling he deeply loved me was ever-present. The sweet, naked innocence of childhood sustained the belief that my grandfather had come back as my guardian angel. In my young mind, he came to protect me, providing warmth, comfort, and love.

Growing into my teens, I found myself in the world of the 1960's. The sweet memories of my night-time friend's love never left me. But I was unprepared for the intensity of those years. Besieged by the senseless brutal war of Viet Nam, I realized I lived in an insane world. Grasping for knowledge and understanding about the human condition, I sought out alternative systems of thought and tried to comprehend the significance of life.

At twenty, I began meditating. Shortly after, I was compelled to go to India where I lived and studied with a Rishi. A man who was widely respected as a spiritual leader. Later, I traveled through Europe, exploring the way other people lived in the world. This was a pivotal time in my life.

In 1972 I came back home to Seattle. I then traveled around the United States lecturing, teaching meditation, and conducting retreats and seminars. Marrying in 1973, I soon had a beautiful daughter. Unfortunately my marriage ended in divorce before her second birthday.

In 1979, under unusual circumstances I met a Tibetan Lama. By the spring of 1980 my daughter and I were living with a Tibetan Lama and his translator. He embraced us as his own family, teaching us the rich traditions of Tibetan Buddhism.

Interested in working with young children, I obtained a Certificate in Early Childhood Education and a BS in Psychology from the University of Oregon, receiving the honors of Summa Cum Laude and Phi Beta Kappa. Later I took graduate course work in Neuroscience and Counseling. I worked in the field of Early Childhood Education, with abused children, and taught classes in parenting.

Remarrying in 1982, my daughter, husband, and I developed strong and healthy ties. We worked hard throughout the 1980's, forming a family and a comfortable lifestyle. All the cultural and spiritual exploration I studied in the past added to my understanding. Yet I didn't need to pursue it any further. I had learned that creation, what we call God, lived within me. All the answers to life were inside myself. I just had to listen!

It was essential that I love myself the way my culture and religion had taught me to love others. This life was a gift, given to me. If I spent my whole life saving others and did not love myself, then I would have served no one. My gifts would have been empty. I learned not to let others, no matter how well meaning, control me. Listening to the voice within, I followed my own path.

In an instant, the 1990's were here. Our daughter, Jennifer, was preparing for college. She was leaving home. While I experienced many feelings of loss, they didn't prevent my thrill at the possibility of having time for myself.

During the first part of my life, I had learned how to meet my needs. Now in my mid-forties, I was free to pursue my dreams. Resolved to make the art of happiness a living reality, I was ready to move into the next half of my life. I wanted to experience all the joy life had to offer. Believing it would be fun to teach meditation again, I set up a class.

In the early part of November 1992, I taught my first meditation class in years. It was delightful. A close friend and I were planning a trip to Venice, Italy in early March. Contented, I watched my life unfold into an arena that was both comfortable and stimulating. Still, *something* was pulling at me.

I was plagued throughout my life with psychic experiences and intuitions. In an effort to elude them, I played down their occurrence and their significance. These experiences seemed to come and go throughout my life without my consent. Unable to recognize their usefulness, I had convinced myself they weren't worth my attention. Now it was time I stop ignoring them.

On January 31, 1993, I experienced an *Alien Abduction.* Nothing could have prepared me for that incident, or the events that followed. My life and my perception changed, in a way that words can only begin to make known.

My goal in writing this book is not to explain, justify, or document the phenomenon of UFOs or their inhabitants. It's not my purpose to convince those who would doubt my sanity, my sincerity, or my intentions. My desire is simply to share a chronicle of personal events that triggered the *remembering* of a long and intimate relationship. A relationship that existed before I was born.

From the moment we are born, we are socialized into our culture of origin. Taught how to experience reality, we learn through the reactions of significant care takers, social institutions, and the relationships we experience. Acceptance by others into our society dictates how we *should* behave, and how we *should* think. Expected to follow these rules, we engage in society's dance, no matter how absurd. Losing sight of whom we are, separate from what society, schools, and parents prescribe, we often leave behind the imagination of childhood. We abandon our inner knowledge to live in the world.

Molded and subsequently defined by this process, we turn away from the essential pathways to our soul. The simple and magical precepts of a child may be a more accurate depiction of the world, than what we as adults might believe. In a child's reality, anything can be real. A young child finds infinite joy, simply participating in the process of discovery. Immersing themselves in the thrill of exploration, they experience their world with a pure heart and an untouched mind.

Like many children, I experienced unusual phenomena in my early years. Those experiences, later overshadowed by my enculturation, were not an acceptable part of the reality I was taught. My memory disregarded many of these wonders and concealed them from my conscious mind.

When I looked into the research on UFOs and *Alien Abductions*, I became aware there were signs throughout my life, marking my relationship to this phenomenon. Of course at the time, there was no way for me to know! Although I was stunned by this *Alien Abduction* in Sisters, Oregon on January 31, 1993, its intrusion into my life made sense. A surge of memories flooded into my conscious mind, like a raging river cutting a path to the sea out of a mountain.

My encounters with UFOs and the resulting memories, changed my perception of myself and the world around me. Everything I *believed* about myself and the world I thought I knew, is no longer relevant. My participation in these events hurled me from a place of security and comfort into the **unknown**. I stood exposed and alone on the edge of a precipice.

We perceive the events in our lives through the filter of our ego. If our perception is based in duality, right or wrong and good or bad, we've allowed our culture to package up our reality and define its parameters. In truth, it's impossible for anyone, beyond the limits of their own experience, to assess the validity of someone else's perception. Yet, if just for a moment we can accept the belief that everything a person experiences is real and true, we have an opportunity. In choosing not necessarily to *believe*, but to *suspend disbelief,* a new understanding may emerge.

Throughout the following chronicle, I lovingly refer to the *Beings* that came to me that night in January as my *friends.* It is here, cloaked in the events of this story, I reveal my participation in the phenomenon known as *Alien Abduction.* Initially, I was deeply concerned about linking myself and my family to the controversial nature of this material. I thought it might be better if I wrote under an assumed name. However, during the process of writing my story, my family and I shared many heartfelt conversations. Compelled by my family's encouragement and the support of close friends, I decided to use my true name.

Although the deeply personal experiences in this book, happened to me exactly as I describe, certain characters have been created to provide a platform for story-telling. Any likeness these characters may have to real persons, other than those identified, is purely coincidental. To protect those involved with my story who wished to remain anonymous, I have altered some characters, locations, and sequence of events.

IT'S TIME TO REMEMBER

CHAPTER ONE:

THE VISIT

"You too must not count overmuch on your reality as you feel it today, since, like that of yesterday, it may prove an illusion for you tomorrow. "
    Luigi Pirandello,
    Six Characters in Search
    of an Author
    (1921),3,tr, Edward Storer

Having spent the last week and a half attending business meetings in Los Angeles and San Francisco, my husband, Mark, and I arrived home exhausted. Our daughter, Jennifer, had moved into a new house just before Christmas, in Sisters, Oregon. Proud of her new home, she wanted us to come for a visit.

Jennifer attended a junior college in Bend, Oregon, about thirty miles from Sisters and worked at a nearby ski resort. Cherishing the beautiful mountains and high desert of Central Oregon, she relished her new surroundings and her new-found freedom. But she, like Mark and me, was still adjusting to her first year away from home. She wanted to see us.

It was late January, and an especially cold winter for

Oregon. Two feet of snow had already fallen over the last week. The conditions for travel were treacherous. To make matters worse, Sisters is located in the middle of the Cascade Mountains. We knew that traveling over the mountains in this weather could be dangerous. Yet, unsure of when we'd get another chance to make the trip, it had to be now. Checking with the weather bureau, I found that we had a window of opportunity. There were no snow flurries or ice storms forecast for the next seventy-two hours. Only mildly relieved, I was still apprehensive. I knew that the weather conditions could change in an instant.

As we began our journey up into the Cascade Mountains, I was rejuvenated by the towering evergreen trees and the small, frozen waterfalls lining the banks of the highway. Embracing the magnificent scene sparked an inner stirring, deep within me.

Breathtaking mountains in all their grandeur hovered thousands of feet above us. Emanating an air of enchantment, the tiny road chiseled it's way, winding through the high peaks and lakes of pristine mountains. Shimmering through the clouds, the sun's brilliance illuminated the glistening whiteness all around us. At this moment, I knew Oregon was my home.

Ten minutes outside of Sisters, we called Jennifer from our cellular phone, to meet us at the lodge where we were spending the night. Moments after Mark and I checked in, Jennifer arrived. As we hugged and kissed we drug our suitcases up two flights of stairs.

Pleasantly surprised, the room was large with high, whitewashed open-beam ceilings, and a southwestern motif. It was much nicer than I'd anticipated. After unpacking we drove to Jennifer's to check out her new home.

Her house was a new mobile home, painted in southwestern colors. Beautifully furnished, it had all the amenities. Glancing into each others eyes, Mark and I affirmed our delight. Silently we reveled in the fact that it was clean!

Strangely, I felt queasy and began to lose my breath. Slowly rising, without saying a word, I walked into the kitchen. Responding with mere nods when spoken to, I allowed the conversation to whirl around me, pretending to participate.

A small garden window over the sink brought in a sweeping sunlight, an expansive meadow, and breathtaking mountains. Placing one hand on each corner of the sink, I leaned into the window, to take in the heavenly views. Mountains and meadows lay silent before me. Standing there mesmerized, I innocently trusted that the beauty of the scene could ease my symptoms.

Leaning further into the window, my gaze was drawn up and fixed on an object about fifty feet above the house, over the meadow. It was a round spherical object with a metallic-silver appearance. It was a UFO! Instantly, I felt like throwing-up.

My intellect tried to rationalize what I was seeing, with what I *believed*. Shock, nausea, then panic surged through my body. All I could think was, "How fast can I get away from this window?"

Quickly, I moved into the family room and sat in front of a small, covered window. I thought, "As long as I can't see what I just saw, I'll be okay." My heart pounded wildly throughout my body and the thought, "I'm okay," kept racing through my mind. Agonizing, minimizing, and working to contain my fear, I made every effort to persuade myself that nothing was happening.

Sitting on a makeshift sofa that doubled as a twin bed, I continued talking with Mark and Jennifer as if nothing had happened. Attributing my delusion to the flu or being overly tired, I thought if I avoided the window I would be all right.

For a few moments I sat holding my stomach and waiting for the feelings to pass. I did everything in my power to negate the reality of what I had just seen and to deny I was experiencing anything. Then thoughts started coming into my mind from somewhere else. They were not my own! Recognizing that *it* was communicating with me, I couldn't believe what was happening.

Emotionally stunned, I didn't know whether to laugh or cry. Impressions and feelings fused into my body and mind, taking the form of thoughts and mental images. *They* advised me that everything was okay. Repeatedly, I was instructed not to be afraid. Desperately, I focused on my family.

Tired, Mark wanted to go back to the lodge and lie down before dinner. As we drove back to the lodge, I looked up. The UFO was still there! *It* tried to calm me telepathically. But I was terrified. Fear and shock emerged and subsided inside me. I tried not to feel, not to think, and not to see that they were there.

I had made reservations for dinner at our favorite restaurant, located in an area outside Sisters. Jennifer's boyfriend was at a family friend's house, watching the Super Bowl. He planned to join us for dinner. As Jennifer and I walked out to the car, to pick him up, I paused for a moment. Leaning against the door, I scanned the sky. I didn't see much of anything. My inner dialog had finally subsided and when we picked up Dan, I engrossed myself in conversation. Together we drove back to the lodge to pick up Mark for dinner.

For a moment I forgot about the metallic, spherical object. But after leaving for the restaurant, I felt someone watching us. Again I scanned the sky, but saw nothing. It had become dark. Huge, gray clouds slowly moved across the night sky. They looked like snow clouds. Arriving at the restaurant, we parked our car about forty feet from the door in an empty, dark parking lot.

Walking into the restaurant through two huge doors, we were welcomed by a small, cozy fire, in a large river rock fireplace. The fire created a golden glow throughout the room. It was a pleasant contrast from the cold darkness outside.

Constructed of natural woods and decorated with American Indian art, the restaurant was lovely. Expansive picture windows arose from the floor to meet thirty-foot vaults, overlooking a small glacier lake. Unfortunately, there were no lights outside to illuminate the inspiring setting. Looking out the window, all I could see were variegated shades of gray.

While ushering us to our table a cordial hostess greeted our arrival. Then, startling even myself, I fell over my feet, the table, and chairs to claim a seat with its back to the window. In my panic, I thought if I put my back to the window I wouldn't see or feel whoever was out there, watching. Making every effort to enjoy each moment, I ordered some wine and took in the conversation. Still, there wasn't a moment I didn't feel a presence, watching us.

When we finished dinner, we started back to the lodge. Darkness had fallen in around us. Satiated and relaxed by the wonderful meal, we drove in silence. The only lights along the road came from whatever businesses might still be open. And, since there were few along that stretch of highway, I was acutely aware of the darkness. Looking up out my window, I couldn't see any stars. The sky was completely black.

Returning to the lodge, we all talked while Jennifer and Dan got into their car. After kissing the kids good night, we stood shivering in the dimly lit parking lot, waving as they drove away. Then Mark and I turned and raced each other up the stairs. Freezing, laughing, and out of breath, we pushed open the door to our room.

Preparing for bed, we giggled about Jennifer and her boyfriend. Dan had been in a hurry when he left the party. So he brought a change of clothes with him for dinner, planning to change in our room. As soon as he walked through the door, he began changing. Talking on and on, he told us stories about a man I had only briefly met. Dan stood unzipping his pants, unaware that he was changing in front of us. Holding back our amusement, Mark and I cast smiles at each other. Now we chuckled with those sweet impressions fresh in our mind.

CHAPTER TWO:

THE DREAM

"We wake from one dream into another dream."
Emerson, "Illusions,"
The Conduct of Life
(1860).

Television normally served as a transition from the stress of the day for us to sleep. But this night was different. For some reason, after changing into our nightclothes we went straight to bed. After we turned off the lights, Mark quickly fell into a deep sleep. Enlivened by the dinner conversation and the joy of seeing Jennifer, I was no longer tired. At home, I would have gone to another part of the house; where I could read, catch up on correspondence, or watch TV. But we weren't at home. All I could do was lie there awake, hoping to fall asleep.

I hadn't mentioned to anyone what I was experiencing. After all, I *believed* it wasn't real. When we left the restaurant, I didn't see anything like a UFO. And, while the night sky was dark and cloudy, I was convinced it was gone. It was all a figment of my imagination. I thanked God it was over! It had passed like the twenty-four-hour flu.

Now the bizarre events of the day were the farthest

thing from my mind. Yet suddenly I was annoyed by a bright light, filtering through the edge of the heavy curtains, covering the sliding glass door to the balcony. Irritated, I began to think the light was responsible for my insomnia. Our room overlooked a snow-covered pool and a small meadow. Since I couldn't sleep, I thought I'd get up to see where the light was coming from. Making every effort not to awaken Mark, I gently pulled back the covers and tiptoed to the sliding glass door. Carefully pulling back the curtains, I peeked out through the glass.

There in front of me, I saw three huge floodlights, streaming down from the tops of the trees around the pool. An image of brilliant blue-white light ignited the snow-covered earth. The dazzling snow, shimmered as it lay silent before me. Light sprinkled through the trees, scattering a soft radiance, illuminating the atmosphere. Reflecting back up into the trees, the brilliance created an illusion of blue-white fire.

The exquisite beauty of the scene was intoxicating. All was right with the world! I stood there entranced by it's dazzling splendor. Feeling a sense of peace, I turned away from the scene and tiptoed back to bed.

A fleeting sense of wonder nagged at my quickly-fading consciousness. Perhaps I should call the office and ask them to turn off the flood lights? Now looking back on that scene, it seems odd that I didn't react differently. At the time, I assumed the lights were there for security.

Crawling back into bed, I gently pulled the covers over me, thinking that I felt better knowing those lights were out there. Glancing over at Mark, I made sure I hadn't awakened him. The digital clock on the nightstand next to him flashed ten-thirty. As my head touched the pillow, I instantly drifted off into that place just before sleep.

Abruptly, in dream-like movements, four men (or what appeared to be men) entered the room. Materializing through the wall and sliding glass door, they appeared in front of me. Dazed, perplexed, and dumbfounded, I couldn't believe what was happening.

Approximately five-feet-eight inches tall, with slight builds, they wore tight-fitting dark, blue body suits. Moving in unison, they advanced toward me. As I lay there in shock, the *Being* closest to me extended what I thought was a very long finger. Then touching my forehead, between the eyes, my head exploded into light.

Luminescent blue-white light pulsated inside me while particles of light burst in the space around me. A strange swirling sensation flooded through me. I tingled from the center of my being out, through every atom in my body, with a feeling unlike any I ever remembered. (Throughout my life, I'd experienced a blue-white light pulsating inside my head. But, it was never associated with anything so shocking, or so I thought.)

Slowly, my body lifted up off the bed in a horizontal position. It moved into a beam of light that just seemed to appear. Moving in unison, the men stood on each side of me, flanking my body without touching me. Somehow, unknown to my conscious mind, the light, the men, and my own volition carried me into a luminescent beam of blue-white radiance.

Entering the light, I felt intoxicated, happy, and safe. In a flash, I found myself walking in dream-like movements, in a silvery looking corridor with rounded walls. My movements languished, but my mind was very much awake. My feet had the sensation of touching what appeared to be the floor. But I was floating. As I moved along the corridor, I was aware of a soft, luminescent light emanating from the upper part of a curve in the wall. Its iridescent quality softly illuminated the silvery, smooth metallic surfaces. I noticed hieroglyphics etched into a doorway as we passed through it. The characters looked familiar, but I couldn't quite make out their meaning. Still, I had the feeling that I knew.

Moving in unison through the doorway, we entered a round room with an examining table in the center. Ushering me to the table, *they* eased off my nightgown. As I lay down on the table, I looked to my right and saw a *female Being* entering the room from another doorway. I didn't know she was female by anything that appeared in her form, it was simply that she *felt* female. Wrapped in a spiral of blue-white radiant light, her form appeared delicate. Emanating a smile toward me, I instantly returned her greetings of warmth and love without any forethought.

I remembered her! She had been in my room at night when I was a small child. It was she who came into my room when I slept, soothing my hair and holding my head. At first, I couldn't make out what she was saying. Her mouth didn't move, but she continued talking to me without speech. In those first moments, her lips did not express a smile. It was more like feelings and impressions, transmitted directly from her mind into mine.

Her thoughts merged into me, having a substance and quality all their own. They appeared as impressions of warmth and joy. She said, "A pleasure to see you my sweet friend." Without any hesitation I responded, "Yes, the pleasure is mine, as well." It was as if we knew each other intimately. Some part of myself had complete knowledge and total recall of all the times we'd been together.

I had always thought my mother came into my room late at night. I had thought my mother gently stroked my hair to say good-night. The *female Being* came over and began stroking my hair and forehead, just as I had remembered. Now I knew it had been she, not my mother.

A luminescent light emanated from the table into my body. The light radiating into me felt cool and soothing. My consciousness seemed to float inches above my body, appearing as a luminescent blue-white light, flitting in and out. I watched what was happening with curiosity.

There were other *Beings* in the room that seemed to be preparing instruments. I knew I had done this before. It was all familiar. A circular beam of light was placed over my body. Shaped like a doughnut, I was in the hole. Starting at my head, it flowed over me. Reaching my feet, the light returned, flowing in the opposite direction. It was cleaning my body.

The light in my head began increasing. Continuing to emanate from the center of my forehead, it now radiated out from my crown. The substance and quality of the light growing inside me, was similar to the light surrounding the *female Being*. Astounded, I suddenly realized that it was exactly the same blue-white light.

The *doctor* came into the room. (I refer to this *Being* as the *doctor* because that is how he feels.) Like the *female Being*, he appears in a spiral of blue-white radiant light. Again, there was no tangible evidence he was male. He only *felt* as though he had male attributes. He greeted me with warmth and love. Naturally, I returned greetings of warmth and love to him. I knew him.

After our initial salutations, my body became rigid, frightened, and then terrified. I wanted to scream out and cry, but I couldn't. My body would not respond. He advanced toward me, as if driven by some duty.

He stood at the edge of the examining table at my feet,

which were slightly parted. Then, a feeling of tremendous cold, like an outrageous north wind, blew through and into my naked, petrified body. A strange tingling sensation engrossed me. I tried to retch, but I couldn't move. I lay there, sick to my stomach. The *doctor* reached down into what seemed like the center of my body. Desperately, I tried to meet the pain before it reached my mind. Instinctively, my body attempted to double over. Again I couldn't move. An icy cold and a strange tingling sensation engulfed me. The light continued, flowing in and out of my poor, terrorized body. The *female Being* continued gently stroking my hair and forehead, soothing me. It was clear she empathized with my feelings of horror. She kept the pain at bay.

The *doctor* pulled an object out of my body, and held it up for me to examine. My first thought was that it looked like a silver Christmas Tree. Then I saw that it was two triangles, piggy-back. The object, four inches in diameter, was made of some sort of alloy. Although it had a smooth metal appearance, it was pliable. I wondered, "If they are taking that *thing* out of me, when had they put it in?"

Lying there cold and exposed, I was stunned. The *doctor* told me that I had to be conscious while these procedures were completed. I focused on the light. The white luminescence would hover over my body one moment, then merge back into it the next.

Assisted by others whom I did not see, the *doctor* worked with speed and precision. After pulling out the triangular object, *they* continued working on my mid-section, forehead, and crown. I don't remember everything occurring on *that* table. But I clearly remember the pro-foundly gripping emotions of terror, shock, and anger. Strangely, my emotions were coupled with boundless surges of joy, love, gratitude, and peace.

The *doctor* and *female Being* conveyed information telepathically to me throughout the procedures. I had no more ova. My cycle was completed. Emanating impressions into my mind that took the form of thoughts, they described everything they were doing. It was as if some part of me fully understood. And I participated with full knowledge, agreeing to it.

When the *doctor* completed his work I felt them say, "It's time to go." It seemed that the timing of everything was critical. The *doctor* told me that the light in my head was now, *"completely activated."* It was no longer necessary for the implant, which *they* had just removed.

Strangely, all my life I'd waited for this moment, to be *awakened* from my earthly sleep. Still, I lay there in terror. This was not the kind of *awakening* I had in mind!

My panic and terror was so real, and so shattering, I thought I would die. These *Beings* took me from a place of safety, and put me on a table. Instruments were placed into my body, seemingly, without my consent. How could *they* just come into my room and take me from my bed? On the other side of my fear, I knew I was in the presence of my own people.

When *they* finished, I sat up and *they* helped me put on my clothes. Shivering from the cold, I was happy to get back into my nightgown. After stepping down from the table, I was led into another part of the ship. I had the feeling this was an area I had not been in before. All the assistants, the *female Being*, and the *doctor* entered the room with me. This was an important moment. Curiously, it felt like an initiation or celebration of some kind.

The *female Being* stood at my right and the *doctor* on my left. Together, we stood in front of a large, curved window, peering out over the mountainous terrain below. While nothing was said, at that moment *I knew.* I *remembered they* were here to help. We stood in silence, looking out over the snow-capped mountains. My mind emptied, everything stopped. Everything I had previously learned about the world I lived in, was of little consequence.

Then, the *doctor* turned to me. Looking into my eyes, mind to mind, he stated with unmitigated clarity, *"It's time to remember."* An intensely powerful force surged into the very core of me, deep into my soul. Having a will of its own, it penetrated further and further piercing all matter of form and thought. Descending into the particles of my very being, I transcended. Finding myself in that place, uniting all creation, I now *remembered.* I had always known this place inside me. I was not what I appeared to be. I was not who I thought I was.

The *doctor* continued, "You were chosen. Your DNA was coded to awaken at this time." Instantly, before I even realized it, the thought, "Bull, find some other sucker," raced through my mind. Continuing without acknowledging my thoughts, he told me to touch people. Thereby, activating those whose time had come to *remember.* It was time to activate those who were ready.

Suddenly my body turned around. There, beyond the doorway, in the room I had just come out of, a young woman stood in her nightgown with long flowing black hair. Her eyes did not blink. They were opened in a dazed, distorted frantic state. The *Beings* who brought me to the ship flanked each side of her. Once she saw me her expression changed to relief, then joy. She knew me! I reached out my hand to hers and together we walked to the examining table. As she lay down, her eyes never left mine. Loving her with my mind, I assured her, easing her fear. She was safe in my care. The *doctor* and others performed procedures on her body while her eyes bathed in my love. The *female Being* stood at her head and lovingly stroked her hair and forehead. I held her hand. *There was no pain.* I knew that this was the way of things. To survive the shock of these events, from the *impressions* of her world, this young woman needed to know she was safe. Fear would only serve to create images of suffering, *where there were none.* When *they* completed their work with her, I helped her with her nightgown. As she gazed into my eyes, I said good-bye with my mind, holding her hand long enough for her to know that I loved her. Immersed in *our* love she was escorted back to her home.

I thought it would be time for me to go. I was ready. But *they* led me into another small room and coerced me into eating some sort of small cake-like food substance. It was only about an inch square. Although I resisted, *they* were insistent. Biting into the food, I was jolted by the terribly bitter taste and odd texture. It was awful. When I finished eating, the *doctor* gently slipped his hand in mine. *They* all stood around fixated on me. *They* were pleased with me. But more than that, *they* appeared to be gloating. I was happy to be with them and felt a sense of elation, deep within my soul.

At the *doctor's* touch, I felt a tremendous warmth and love coursing through my body. The love expressed to me was more profound than I have ever *remembered* knowing. We began to talk with our minds back and forth, like lovers who had not seen each other in a long time. Seizing the moment, we caught up on all the things that had happened in the time we'd been apart. He instructed me. I knew who I was and where I belonged. We had never really been apart.

We walked along the corridor in dream-like movements. Accustomed to the sensations, it all felt natural, comfortable, and more real than what I had perceived as my life. *I was home.*

From the corridor we descended into a chamber that opened with a swirling motion of light. Responding to our thought, the ship was alive. An immense luminescent blue-white light streamed down, like a rushing waterfall of light, cascading without sound, down to earth. Continuing to hold hands, we entered the light.

Gently floating downward, my arms, as if experiencing no gravity, lifted slowly over my head. My nightgown billowed as a soothing wind blew all around me. Together we drifted ever so softly onto the balcony outside my room. Merging through the sliding glass door, we materialized inside the room. Everything I experienced was normal and natural.

I stood there with the *doctor* looking at Mark as he lay sleeping on the bed. It was as if he wanted me to make notes of these moments, so I would remember these events. There was nothing but emptiness where I had previously lain waiting to fall asleep. Glancing at the digital clock on the nightstand, I noticed it was four-thirty. Still holding hands, we walked together toward the bed. I looked over into my *friend's* eyes one more time and he in mine. I didn't want to leave him. I wanted to stay with him and my home.

Waves of warm liquid light flowed over my head and down into my body. Smiling in his mind, the sweet warmth emanating from his being filled me with joy. My heart knew, I would never be apart from my *friends* again. The dream of *this world* could not keep us apart.

As he held up the covers for me to slip into bed, I looked over at Mark. I giggled like a child thinking, "Mark always thinks he's aware of everything." My *friend* acknowledged my thoughts with regard and attention. As I slipped into bed, he gently pulled the covers over me and tucked the excess blanket around my neck, under my chin. Lying there with my eyes closed, I smiled to myself. Feelings of peace and a sense of oneness with the universe embraced my being. Gently stroking my hair one last time, as if to say good night, my *friend* quietly slipped away.

The next morning I awoke to feelings of shock and horror. What had happened to me? Was it real? It sure felt real. Was it a dream, a nightmare? Was I going out of my mind? I sat up in bed holding my face in my hands, attempting to assess whether I was real. My body was sitting in the bed, in the room, at the lodge, where I had gone to bed the previous night. What had happened to me? Trying to tell Mark I had a terrible nightmare, he interrupted me before I could continue. He didn't want to hear about it. The words, *"It's time to remember,"* echoed through my mind.

Confused, disoriented, and horrified, I wondered what had happened to me? My body felt raw inside. I felt raped. At the same time, I experienced feelings of warmth, joy, and love. Still, I tried to forget.

Like a rape victim, my first thoughts were denial. Deny! Deny! Deny! It never happened. It must have been something I ate, like Scrooge in *A Christmas Carol.* I felt shell shocked. My demeanor was wary, vigilant, and pensive. With all my mind's effort I could not forget what had happened that night. I felt nauseous. Yet, at the same time, touched by something awesome and powerfully magnificent.

Although I told myself it was just a *bad dream*, the memory of this strange experience permeated my every thought. I kept feeling the *doctor* tell me, *"It's time to remember."* Remember *what*, I thought. What had I forgotten? How can I forget a dream like that? It was too strange. It was too startling to forget. How does one fabricate something so fantastic? I couldn't imagine! This event was too outrageous to forget, but believe me, I was going to try.

Pressuring me to get dressed, Mark was unaware of what was happening to me. Unable to utter a word, I was dumbfounded. I thought, "I can't talk about this to anyone. They'll think I've lost my mind. I'm not even sure I haven't lost my mind. But, I feel Okay! I've spent my whole life trying to make sense of this world and then this has to happen."

Pulling myself together, I dressed for breakfast. We were meeting Jennifer, Dan, and his parents at a nearby restaurant. I needed to switch my focus. So I did.

Breakfast was fun and soon we were all hugging good-bye and talking about the next time we'd get to see each other. Walking out of the restaurant we kissed our sweet daughter one more time, and left for home. Forgetting for a moment about my bizarre *dream,* I looked forward to the scenery along the highway, through those magnificent mountains.

As Mark and I walked back to the car, we felt a sense of warmth and love toward each other. This was one of those special moments. We've worked through a lot with one another, and here we were on the other side of all that effort with a beautiful daughter and a good life.

On our way out of town we passed the lodge where we'd spent the night. I was instantly reminded of my *dream.* Glancing over toward the meadow and the pool sitting undisturbed in the front of the lodge, *I saw no flood lights.* There were only a few lodge pole pines dispersed around the beautifully groomed grounds.

Overwhelmed by the memories of the previous night, I hardly said anything. I sat there dazed as Mark drove us down the mountains. I allowed myself to be.

CHAPTER THREE:

THE AFTER SHOCK

*"All changes, even the most longed for, have
their melancholy; for what we leave behind us
is a part of ourselves; we must die to one life
before we can enter into another!"*
> Anatole France
> The Crime of Sylvestre Bonnard
> (1881), 2,tr. Lafacadio Hearn

Mark and I drove down through those breathtaking
mountains toward home in silence. Wrapping my coat
around my body, up to my chin, I tried to protect myself
from the cold and whatever else out there that had entered
my world. Resting the side of my head against the cold
window, I slumped down into the corner between the seat
and the door.

Peering out through the window, my eyes acknowledged the magnificent snow-laden trees, lining the
highway. The serene beauty was a perfect backdrop for my
shock. Immersed in the memory of my *dream*, there wasn't
room in my mind for anything else.

Where did this *dream* come from? What dark secrets
of my soul had I suppressed that were now surfacing? Had
I lost contact with reality? Knowledgeable and comfortable

with myself, I couldn't imagine where this *dream* had come from.

Once home, I was exhausted and dazed. Thinking my friends would believe I was delusional, I was resolved to share my *dream* with no one. Unsure myself of what was going on, I was unwilling to expose myself to others.

After we unpacked, Mark seated himself in front of the TV while I prepared dinner. When we went to bed that night, I felt an unbelievable terror. I lay there awake, unable to sleep, fearing the recurrence of my *dream*.

Denying my *dream*, I tried to absorb myself in day to day life, or what I had *believed* was my life. It wasn't possible. Life as I had known it, didn't exist. In spite of the overwhelming feelings, I took comfort in thinking I could keep my *dream* a secret. Unfortunately, even that didn't last.

A few days later, I received a call from a good friend, Peggy Snicale. Peggy and I had known each other for eight years. We had a genuine respect and love for one another, and shared a deeply personal relationship. Peggy had experienced some unusual phenomenon herself. Still, I was apprehensive about telling her my *dream*.

Frightened my *dream* might escape my lips, I clung tightly to her words. As I listened attentively, she told me what was happening in her life. Her words filtered through my thoughts, while notions of telling her fought back and forth inside my mind. After exhausting other topics of conversation, I broke down. Carefully, I shared the details of my *dream* and the events that had followed.

I wanted to believe it was all just a nightmare. That at any moment, I would awaken and my life would be back to normal. To my astonishment, Peggy's silence on the other end of the phone wasn't followed by shock or surprise.

Amazingly, she told me a UFO was sighted in Oregon a couple of nights earlier. I had remembered hearing something about it on the news. Together we calculated the night. My heart sank into my stomach. It was the night my *dream* occurred. Peggy told me that she had read about a phenomenon known as *Alien Abduction*, and urged me to read a book titled, *Communion* by Whitley Strieber. She assured me that others had had similar experiences.

When we finally got off the phone, it was late. Emotionally drained, I didn't want to think about it anymore. Peggy had affirmed my experience as something other than a *dream*. On one level her support was comforting. Yet on another, her knowledge of *Alien Abductions* forced me to acknowledge that my *dream* could be real!

The concurrent dilemma I faced, was that the contact my *friends* had made with me on January 31st, had not ended that night. My relationship with these *Beings* was ongoing. Confining myself to the house, I tried to assess what was happening.

After going to bed at night, I'd lie motionless in the dark, my body rigid with fear. Opening my eyes as wide as possible, I'd peer out from under the covers into the blackness. Panicking from time to time, I'd feel them in the shadows, waiting for me to drift off to sleep. The feeling of being watched was always with me. Denial didn't provide a way out.

Compelled to look at the world in a new way, I wondered if my *friends* were inter-dimensional. I sensed their presence with me at all times. While I couldn't see them in the same way I see people in the third dimension, I could feel them. Imparting knowledge to me, they were always kind and loving. Often they made comical remarks about my make-up and hair. Their playful humor and infinite love flowed into me, soothing my anxiety. My *friends* gave me a feeling of absolute acceptance and unconditional love. I no longer focused on my flaws. Now, looking into the mirror I *saw* my incredible perfection. Even in the light of deficiencies, I felt an immense self-acceptance that increased with each passing day. These new perceptions unveiled the profound splendor of my *real nature*. Often I felt my *friends* touch me. But these were not new experiences. I *remembered* the many times throughout my life they had occurred. Yet they had never occurred with such intensity and awareness.

Initially, I was apprehensive about reading the literature on UFOs and *Alien Abductions*. Concerned it might affect my thinking, I didn't want anything to taint my view, or how I chose to perceive these events. As time passed, I recognized a fathomless inner strength growing within me and I knew that nothing and no one could sway me from my own perception. So I decided to look into the literature.

Because of the overwhelming nature of these events, I was initially uncomfortable around groups of people, even close friends. Yet compelled to investigate the literature, I forced myself to drive to the local mall, hoping that a bookstore there might have some material on *Alien Abductions*.

Arriving at the mall, I found it hauntingly quiet. Deeply relieved, I saw only a few people redoing mannequins in the store windows. With brisk strides I strolled along the huge, deserted walkways, adorned with tall, tropical plants and wooden benches. As my footsteps echoed throughout the building, my body was soothed by the warm sunlight filtering through the skylights. Propelled by a sense of anxious curiosity, I headed straight for the bookstore. There I searched for a category fitting UFO sightings and *Alien Abductions.* Outwardly I expressed self-assurance. Inwardly, I was self-absorbed. I didn't want to relate to anyone. Help from a salesperson was the last thing I wanted. Yet a bored looking clerk kept asking me if I needed anything. Finally after an unsuccessful search, I gave up and accepted his offer.

The clerk, a good looking young man, stood behind a huge traditional, carved wooden counter. Telling him I was looking for the section on UFOs, I asked if he'd point me in the right direction. Staring into my eyes, he looked as if he wanted to ask why. Then he came out from behind the counter. Guiding me to the back of the store, he pointed to a small section. Thanking him, I avoided his gaze. He walked back to his place behind the counter.

Foolishly, I had the feeling that everyone knew what was happening to me, like the first time I had sex. At that time, I thought everyone knew I was no longer a virgin, just by the way I walked. Now in my mind, I saw an image of myself carrying one of those sandwich signs that read, "This woman thinks she talks to aliens and sees spaceships." I even dressed in a way that made me feel protected, wearing my full length leather coat, which completely hid my body. It gave me the feeling, if only an illusion, of sanctuary.

Drawn suddenly out of my reverie, I leaned down to look at the books on the shelf. As I stood there, I realized there were only four. Looking around at the shelves close by, I was surprised to see comic books. Perusing the covers of the books in front of me, I looked for intelligent commentaries, personal experiences, and/or documented works.

Still under the impression that those involved with the UFO phenomenon were somehow mentally insufficient, I assumed the literature would be full of quackery. I picked up the four books on the shelf and took them to the counter, hoping they might provide some answers!

Reading the books, I realized that I had experienced many of the exact same incidents others described. I understood their terror. Still, it was reassuring to know that there were others living through similar circumstances.

Touched by *something* beyond, what I believed to be real, I was profoundly shaken. There was no way to deny these experiences, but they were still too much to believe.

The books I read revealed sobering accounts of other's *remembering*. Momentarily, they provided relief from my feelings of separation; relief from the world I was born. Still confusion and anger would surge, oscillating between intense joy and bliss. Barraged with these powerful emotions, I felt on the brink of a great discovery. I was thrilled. Yet it was difficult to reconcile the events on *that* examining table with the extraordinary feelings of love.

Waking up that morning on February 1st, the world I had known had vanished. I found myself in unseen worlds. Worlds that were not only familiar, but comfortable. *I was home.* In spite of the knowledge that I had known these inner dimensions all my life, I was terrified. My mind couldn't remember *how* I knew them, or when I had forgotten. There were moments I felt on the brink of insanity, torn between unseen worlds one minute and the world of my senses the next.

Feeling like a moth being slowly drawn into a flame, I felt an unrelenting terror. I was completely out of control.

Everything I had believed about myself had literally disintegrated. Nothing I remembered about my childhood or past seemed real. It was completely wiped away. I went to bed on January 31st, thinking I was one person. When I awoke, I was someone else! During this time I entertained fleeting thoughts of suicide. I felt trapped. If I couldn't protect myself from these *Beings*, maybe the only way out was death. For a moment, I thought that if I killed myself, I would be cheating them. For a fleeting moment, I felt as if my life had become immersed in some absurd science fiction film. Maybe they were body snatchers?

As quickly as those thoughts arose, feelings of warmth and love surged into me. A sweet loving laughter filled my soul, showing me that my life was precious. I was loved. It was I who had chosen to be here! My flirtation with suicide extinguished itself. The loving knowledge of my life's purpose floated into me through feelings and impressions from my *friends*. In my youth, I'd always felt like an observer from another place. Now, I knew why!

My *friends* explained that the only purpose for life, is the pure joy of experiencing *itself*. All I had to do was sit back and let my life unfold. All I had to do was let it happen. The world my body was born into had lost it's hold.

Images and memories of my *friends* swept through my mind. All those experiences touching me so deeply throughout my life made sense. I *remembered* the first time I had that paralyzing feeling, at age three. My fragmented experiences of blue-white radiant light and psychic phenomena all fit together. I knew that all these unusual experiences were connected to this one, my *friends*. I had never been alone. Nor was I alone now. And now *remembering,* I would never feel separate from my *friends* again. All my deep inner, child-like perceptions of miracles and angels were affirmed.

Permeating my mind, my *friends* were loving, jovial, warm, and kind. Whom I spoke to, whom I contacted, and how I related to others was directly related to *them*. With my mind now aware of its connection with theirs, I received incredible knowledge. A silver thread of light passed through me, uniting me with them, and all creation.

Remembering, I was aware that there was never a time I didn't experience these impressions. Beams of luminescent, blue-white light, and the radiant light now ablaze in my head had awakened me many times from sleep. As a child I had learned not to talk about these things. They were not acceptable. Yet they were a part of me.

Now I *saw* that nothing can impede the inevitable flow of life from its' natural tendency, to unfold. Each event in my life was synchronized. Everything occurred exactly as planned, *at it's appointed moment.*

When it was clear to me that these experiences were linked to my inner growth, I went to Peralandra, which is a book store that caters to inner awareness and personal well-being. There I was able to find books on *Extraterrestrials* and the *Alien Abduction* phenomenon, which shed light on the spiritual aspects of these encounters. While none of the books I read expressed the same feelings I experienced with my *friends,* they provided a more holistic, inclusive view.

I had made plans with my friend Maggie Matoba, to travel to Italy in early March. As a travel agent, she had gotten a well-priced package to Italy and invited me to go along. We were thrilled at the prospect of traveling together. Maggie was warm and lovable. No matter where we were or what we were doing, we had a good time.

Having both been raised in multi-cultural environments, we shared similar childhood experiences. The best part of our relationship was that we focused on joy.

Realizing there was no way I could hide these experiences from Maggie, through eight days of travel, I arranged a meeting. Since we often met to discuss the plans of our trip, I figured if I felt uncomfortable, I didn't have to tell her. At a small cafe in downtown Eugene, I chose my words carefully. Crouching toward her ear, I carefully whispered the contents of my *dream* and the events that had followed.

Maggie listened patiently. While not knowing a lot about these kinds of experiences, she had known friends who had shared similar incidents. Maggie had studied American Indian mysticism, practiced meditation and was aware of unusual phenomena in her own life. She responded with wonder to my *dream*.

In spite of all my emerging memories and awareness, I often found myself breaking down in tears. The inherent insight, the boundless knowledge, and the overwhelming joy did not dispel my *other* feelings. These experiences were not socially acceptable!

CHAPTER FOUR:

THEIR RETURN

"Only the heart can see beyond the veil;
beyond the phenomenal worlds of our
senses, to what is real and what is true. "
Joy S. Gilbert

I awakened the 11th day after my *dream,* out of control. Feeling I had lost sight of reality, I remembered that the only way out of my pain was to go through it. I began to cry.

The realization that I had no idea who I was, was a living reality. Mourning the death of my perception, I was desperate for answers. Yet there was no one I knew who had experienced anything like this. Resigning myself to the **unknown**, I allowed myself to feel. There was no reason to pull myself together. What did it matter? Fighting these feelings was senseless. There was nothing to do but ride them out. Like everything, I knew they would pass. But who would I be when they did?

Early February, it had been snowing on and off for days. But today the roads were clear and I was forced to go out for groceries. Making it down our steep driveway to the closest grocery store, I wandered through the aisles of food,

looking for the items I needed. Suddenly, I became aware
of a feeling I had had before. Someone else was looking
out into the world through my eyes. I felt lighthearted.
S*omething* else had taken control. That *something* lived
with the knowledge of its vastness. It was aware of its
interconnectedness with all creation. I experienced a feeling
of *Oneness* with all things. I watched, like an observer from
another place, as my consciousness flowed in and out of
everything.

Later that afternoon I was preparing dinner when I
thought my friend Lauren might shed some light on these
events. Lauren had been a good friend for many years. We
went to school together. I thought if anyone would be open
to these apparitions, it would be her.

Attempting to soothe my poor bewildered ego, I called
her. As I shared the details of my *dream,* I told her that after
the events on January 31st my *friends* hadn't gone away.
They were always with me. Light danced around me while
little stars flashed and burst before my eyes. My mind
began to swirl and again I burst into tears.

There was a dead silence on the other end of the
phone. Then Lauren tried to fix me with her words, as if I
were broken. She suggested that I not tell anyone. While
I'm certain her intention was to protect me, her solution to
my dilemma had nothing to do with me. I let it go. Her
response confirmed my original feelings, I had to rely on
myself.

Mark came home from work while Lauren and I were
still talking on the phone. Seeing I was having a difficult
day he maintained a low profile. After I hung up the phone,
a loud silence rang throughout the house.

Out of respect for him, I hadn't yet shared the events of
my *dream.* In return, he'd just accepted that I was going

through *something*. Without questioning or judging, he simply loved me. We went to bed early that night and I cried in his arms.

Mark worked throughout the years of our marriage, learning how to love me. Knowing it wasn't necessary to take responsibility for my pain, he simply allowed me to be who I was. Responding with concern, I knew he was there. Yet I appreciated his distance. There was nothing he could do to help. No one outside myself could shed light on what was happening.

Intuitively, I had known this was coming. Having experienced psychic perceptions throughout my life, I had felt something brewing. Before, I had always made certain these premonitions didn't control my life. When I had visions, I examined them intellectually. If I felt strong about them, I followed them. Now it seemed I had no intellect nor judgment. They were the illusion and the illusion was gone! A veil had lifted midst the worlds I thought I knew, and the worlds I now *remembered.* My memory flowed back and forth between them.

By the following morning the emotions of the previous day had subsided. I felt a child-like innocence and vulnerability. Looking out through the window, I delighted in the new snow that had fallen during the night. Enchanted by its dazzling beauty, I thrilled at the two foot drifts outside my door. Gazing out over the garment of snow covering the earth, I felt a sense of joy and self-assurance.

The turbulent emotions of yesterday transformed into open resignation. Whether my *dream* was real or imaginary didn't matter anymore. Its impact on my life was profound! Ecstatic about the snow, I planned a day of pampering myself, first by starting a cozy fire, and then by placing my face in a good book.

Mark and I followed our typical morning rituals: we watched the news, Mark showered and shaved, while I prepared breakfast. Sharing a few quiet moments, we sipped our coffee and talked about buying a home in the country. There was no discussion of the preceding day. It was clear these events couldn't be understood, at least not with my intellect. This was too fantastic and unbelievable. I couldn't comprehend how I'd react if someone shared these events with me. Feeling any ill will toward Lauren was ridiculous. She was a good friend. I was having a difficult time believing it was happening to me. Yet, it was!

Mark left for work and I took a long, hot shower. Realizing my housekeeper would arrive at 10'o clock, I made sure I had enough time for my morning meditation. I started a small fire in our brick fireplace, which enhanced the cozy feeling of our living room. The house was quiet. I unplugged the phone and settled into our dark green, overstuffed sofa. Momentarily glancing over the living room, I reveled in its high vaulted ceilings and huge windows. A tremendous sense of peace came over me.

Our home was new but the windows were arched at the top, giving the room an old, traditional feeling. The extensive vaults and expansive windows brought in a soft, natural light. Gazing through the windows into the trees, I watched as they gently swayed in the wind. The accumulated snow lightly dusted the atmosphere with a shimmering whiteness. The dark, rich, green firs appeared magnificent against the thickly laden snow, drooping over the top of each bough.

In that peaceful and quiet setting, thoughts of war, famine, earthquakes, flooding, and disease passed through my mind. However, choosing to cherish and savor the moment, I put them aside. There were always those images of suffering in the world that too often served to keep me from experiencing joy. As I looked out into the world, I saw nothing but beauty, perfection, and harmony. I closed my eyes and began to meditate.

Within moments, the blue-white radiant light began to emerge, pulsating inside my head. Unconcerned by its presence, it felt natural, comfortable, and peaceful. As I continued to meditate, the light's brilliance increased. Light streamed into the crown of my head and poured over my body like a liquid radiance, flowing down from somewhere above me.

Suddenly my *mind* saw over our house the same spherical, metallic ship that had appeared on January 31st, in Sisters. Flooding down from the center of the sphere, a beam of light flowed into me. My head was opened from its center and I saw *clearly* with my mind.

Making every effort to maintain control, I respectfully acknowledged their presence. Then with my mind I said, "This is not a good time for you to be here. My housekeeper will be here soon. You should go." Emanating a warm, sweet, and kind laughter, the impressions flooding into my mind flowed out from *a choir of Beings.* Communicating from the center of the light, *they* emitted a sweet melodious quality of unison. Assuring me that I needn't be concerned about my housekeeper, *they* told me, "You won't think of her again until the door bell rings."

Speaking to me as if I were a child, *they* told me I was theirs and not my mother's. *They* went on to say, "You are in this world, but not of it." Listening to their sweet melodious emanations with love pouring into me through the light, my life made sense. As Joy it was my function to be their joy on Earth. **The purpose of all existence is**

simply for the expression of joy and bliss.
They continued, "When all the good things happened
in your life, we were with you." *They* told me *they* were in
my dreams as a child, and at that instant I *remembered* the
dreams with the man in the fedora hat. Teaching me
through my dreams, *they* had revealed the beauty and
perfection of creation. Then calling forth a dream *they* had
given me twelve years ago, I was instantaneously immersed
in its images.

In the flash of a second, I watched the dream unfold
exactly as I'd remembered. It was like watching a movie,
except I was consciously participating in the experience as
it happened. Twelve years earlier, this dream had been
horrifying. These visions, vast and consuming, now
engulfed me. Penetrating deep into my very cells, a
transmission of knowledge occurred.

The dream sequence took place in Berkeley,
California, near the University of California. A good friend
of mine owned a huge, old, beautiful home near the
University's campus. Nora Goldstein, a widow and
Professor, insisted I stay with her while attending seminars
at the University. Sharing the same interests in child
welfare and diverse cultures, we had a special friendship.
(Oddly when this dream occurred I had just returned from a
seminar at the University of Berkeley. I had stayed in
Nora's home.) In the dream, I was staying at Nora's. After
a day of lectures I had returned to her home in the early
evening. Finding no one there, I decided to take a walk.

It was late September and the smells of fall hung in the
chilly evening air. Feeling a burst of energy, I grabbed a
sweater and pushed open the huge, imposing front door. As
I leaped down the stairs of that majestic old house, I gazed
straight ahead just in time to catch sight of the sun setting

over the San Francisco skyline, off in the distance. The sunlight, now fading away, turned the day into dusk. The only sound I heard were my comfortable old boots hitting the pavement. Although I knew that smog changed the colors of the setting sun, as it's rays filtered through the polluted atmosphere, it didn't detract from the beauty of that moment. The muted shades of reds and oranges filtered through the buildings, creating a glow around them. The light sparkled through the trees against the back drop of ensuing darkness. A slight breeze suddenly released golden orange and red leaves. Fragmenting my view, they danced before my eyes in slow motion, gently swirling down to earth.

Suddenly I heard a commotion. As my attention was drawn down a street to my right, I saw the silhouettes of five people and heard a garbled mumbling. They stood leaning over a heaping form lying in the middle of the street. At first, I couldn't see what they were doing. But feeling a sense of urgency, I turned down the street and began walking toward them. The dark contours that defined their bodies looked up, acknowledging my approach. Closer, I realized that the object lying in the street was a body. Now, concluding there was a crime in progress, I ran faster, toward the scene.

The body on the ground wasn't moving. The contoured forms hovering over it appeared to be searching through it's clothing. As I ran faster a fleeting thought caught my minds attention, "What would I do once I got there?" Then I thought, "What does it matter? I have to do something." I began yelling for help.

Porch lights flicked on and I could see the outline of people standing in their doorways as they watched me screaming down the street. The warm light from their houses created a soft glow around their bodies as they stood safe on their porches. Then, I heard a man's voice yell out from the darkness that he'd called 911. Upon reaching the scene, I saw four young men and a young woman crouched around a body. They appeared to be teenagers. Spewing out obscenities, they shouted at me in defiance. "This is our neighborhood and we can do whatever we want. You have no power here, lady." I looked directly into their eyes and said nothing. Continuing, now calm and confident, they told me, "No stupid cops are going to do anything." They sauntered away, unconcerned, each in a different direction.

A woman lay there on her side, in a fetal position. Her long dark hair flowed out everywhere, concealing her face. A pool of blood had formed next to the mid-section of her body. I stood there watching as blood streamed out from the center of her limp and lifeless form. Then leaning down, I gently brushed her tangled hair aside, thinking I would check her vitals. Jolted, I jumped back! Too stunned to move, I let the other people now gathering help her.

Dumfounded, I stared down at myself, wondering who I was as I stood there! Having always been terrified of knives, it seemed ironic that I was watching myself die of a wound most likely inflicted by a knife. I stood there, paralyzed, not knowing what to do. It was as if I were trapped in some other dimension. In the distance, I heard the sounds of approaching sirens. They would be too late.

I remembered how terrified I'd been twelve years ago. Now I felt different. Instead of horror, I was suddenly filled with adoration toward the woman/myself, as she lay there bleeding. Previously, I stood paralyzed in terror and watched her die. Now, I knelt down onto the cold hard pavement. As my skirt drenched with blood, I felt the sharp pieces of broken pavement pierce the skin on my upper thigh. Then placing her head in my lap, I embraced her. Rocking her back and forth like a child, I softly whispered over and over again, "There is nothing to fear." Holding her head and soothing her hair, I watched as the blood drained out of her.

Suddenly she was gone. Feelings of joy and laughter filled me. I began to laugh at all those things I'd believed important. Loneliness was no longer an issue, there was no such thing. Death was no longer a reality, where would I go? Going deep into *that place* within myself, I *remembered*.

Peace and joy came over me. What I had perceived as death no longer existed. There is no death! There is nothing to fear in life, because life *is* creation. And the primary goal of creation is expansion and growth. Nothing is ever lost. Everything is a part of the whole. Death is an illusion, it doesn't exist. How ludicrous my identification with my form, my body, suddenly seemed. This dream we call our life is just another experience with the sole purpose of enhancing and expanding a dynamic and ever-changing universe.

Like going to the theater, we buy a ticket to watch a movie. The purpose is to take our awareness somewhere else for an hour or two, allowing us to partake in experiences different from our everyday life. In the movie we call our life, we become whom-ever we choose. When our role is completed, we merge into the core of creation, never losing anything of ourselves. Whether we remember or not, we were and still are the essence of creation. At the end of our performance, we bring all the experiences, feelings, memories, and impressions of our life with us.

We become that much more than we were in the beginning. Recognizing my time as *Joy* was less than an instant, I laughed to myself for thinking it was more. A Tibetan Lama once told me, "We live in this world as long as it takes for a butterfly to land on the tip of a needle, and then fly away." Now I understood. *My death* now secure in my memory, the light continued pouring into me. All that was necessary was to be happy. There was *nothing* to accomplish and *nothing* to do. The light turned into a golden brilliance and fused into me. Their love and sweet melodious choir-like intonations, instructed me. "Feel everything that comes through you. Do not hold feelings inside you. Allow your emotions to flow through you, feeling everything. The feelings are not who you are, but only through them can you know what is real in this world. Everything you feel is a part of the experience of life. All you need to do is feel, experience, and let go. Like the river flows to the ocean, the feelings and experiences of life flow through you, to your soul." In parting, *they* said, "Tell people we are here, we are real, and we are not here to harm them. Record everything."

In a flash *they* were gone. Immersed in a gentle radiance, I sat there with the door bell ringing. Drawn back into the physical world, I answered the door. My housekeeper stood there smiling. I greeted her, gave her some last minute instructions, and retreated into my office.

I thought, "I don't want anyone to know I'm having these experiences." How in the world would I tell people *they* were here? I wanted to forget the whole thing. Yet, there was no way for me to forget any of it. Although stunned, I was left with feelings of great joy and a sense of divine intervention. (I was never again fearful of death or knives.)

My *friends* had told me to record everything. Still, incredibly shaken by all these events, my task to record became an obsession. In the weeks that followed I worked at my computer, avoiding anything outside my house and facing my *remembering* alone.

One evening after dinner, I went in to shut off the computer before going to bed. The file was gone! I sat there for a moment looking at the screen trying to bring it up from the hard drive. Unsuccessful, I tried to bring it up from the floppy disk. Nothing was there! I didn't feel upset, although I had lost many notes. What had happened? Why weren't the other files gone? Why was it just that file on both the hard drive and the disk?

I thought about all the problems I'd experienced with electrical appliances and watches over the years. Then I thought that this was not what my *friends* had in mind. I stopped frantically writing everything down and began to *feel*. As time went on things became much clearer. Again I sat at my computer.

These events hadn't just appeared. But it was only now that I was fully *remembering*. I was charged with an energy that raced through my soul. Through the emotions of life, I touched what is true for me. I am here on Earth for the pure joy of exploration, to expand my awareness, thereby expanding all creation. Choosing my worlds, I have the opportunity to participate in different life experiences. There is really only *One* of us here, and my *friends* wanted me to *remember*.

I am part of a beautifully orchestrated creation. My *friends* are here and always have been, to help me *remember* my true fortune. In order to experience this world, I chose to forget who I was. But I have never been forgotten. We are all in the mind of creation, and being in that mind, all our deepest dreams are heard, felt, and lived out.

CHAPTER FIVE:

THE PROFESSIONALS

*"How few things can a man measure with the tape of
his understanding! How many greater things might he
be seeing in the meanwhile."*
Thoreau, Journal, Feb. 14, 1851.

My *dream* memories engrossed my every thought. I
experienced the rational world of form and thought one
minute, then found myself plunged into unseen worlds the
next. My mind expanded, then dissolved. Teetering
between intense feelings of shock and profound states of
ecstasy, the one element that remained constant was my
friends.

Eventually, the terror gave way and I became
comfortable in those states of awareness. But it was
difficult in those early days to grasp what was happening.
Realizing the potentially negative reaction of clinical
professionals, I tried to deal with my feelings alone. Still, I
desperately wanted support. I wanted some authority to tell
me I wasn't crazy.

My rational mind tried to cling to the *dream* construct.
But my *dream* was more real than any experience I had ever
known. My *belief* served no purpose. It had no meaning.
These experiences were impossible to even think about, let

alone assess. Their blaring nature gave me no rest. Leaving me no alternative, I had to face them. Hungry for insight, I examined the available literature. Bringing home stacks of books and articles from the university and public libraries, I was astounded by the numbers of people who had similar experiences. They included: doctors, scientists, psychologists, psychiatrists, police officers, pilots, homemakers, celebrities, utility workers, and even high ranking government officials. My investigation uncovered many documented accounts, providing me a glimpse into others' experiences.

An array of circumstances just like mine, existed in most accounts. Whirling my rational mind, they fit one by one into place. Some similarities were: seeing a ray or beam of light; an examining table; physically probed and/or ova harvesting in females and sperm collection in males; missing time; events beginning in early childhood; psychic phenomena; scars appearing from unknown origins; memories or evidence of superior surgical techniques and procedures; implants placed in the ear, nose, brain through the eye, and in some cases just under the skin tissue in the arm, leg, abdomen, or hand; and the showing of dreams. (The literature suggests that visions or dreams are planted into the minds of participants to elicit some type of undetermined response.)

After poring over the literature, I realized that each person's experience reflected more who they were and their state of mind, than any determined value that could be placed on my *friends*. Still my investigation helped my rational mind substantiate the conclusion: there was something really going on! Otherwise, why would all these unrelated individuals, with various childhood backgrounds in different parts of the world, whom I didn't even know, have identical elements within their experiences? There were many theories, but none of them fit into my perception.

Although I was delighted that such astute investigators had devoted their time to the study of UFOs and the *Alien Abduction* phenomenon, most of the literature, revealing first hand accounts, was written by researchers. So, I didn't feel I was getting an accurate picture of how others adapted. How did they integrate these events into their lives?

In addition to my quandary, the literature seemed to have a generally negative tone. It disturbed me that so many accounts converged on the traumatic and the invasive; particularly since I felt a profound love from, and for my *friends*. Even the widely used terminology *Alien Abduction* suggested being terrorized and kidnapped.

My usual approach to coping with problems was to seek out support, clinical help. Initially, I hoped to find a clinician who, whether they believed me or not, would be open to the possibility.

My first contact with a therapist was with my friend Lauren. When I told her, the deafening silence on the other end of the phone and her loud monotone voice rang loud and clear. Speaking to me as if I were a child, her words were deliberate. She assumed I'd experienced a *break with reality* and told me to keep my experiences secret.

Unwilling and unable to deny my experiences, relentlessly I pursued that one person, whoever they might be, who might affirm my sanity!

My *friends* repeatedly told me to call a psychologist I had known several years ago, whom I shall call Dr. Patricia Shields. This was only the beginning of their day-to-day guidance in my life. Finally I gave in and called.

Patricia was a local psychologist I had worked with several years before on a family matter. When I called, I told her I had experienced what is commonly referred to as an *Alien Abduction*. I asked if she had any knowledge of this phenomenon. Assuring me that she did, I was thrilled at the possibility of talking to her. Meeting her the following week, I shared my *dream* and detailed the phenomena that had followed.

Patricia was nonchalant as I recounted the events of January 31st. She told me that she'd read a book titled, *Communion*. Apparently, after seeing the author Whitley Strieber on the Johnny Carson show, she was compelled to read his book. Since then, she *believed* this was a legitimate phenomenon.

Patiently, I waited to hear if she had done any other research. Although surprised that *Communion* was her only exposure to the subject, I trusted her and continued to share my experiences.

Patricia was perceivably shaken by what I told her. Leaving her office, I looked into her eyes as I extended my hand. She avoided my gaze. Then sarcastically she muttered under her breath, loud enough for me to hear, "Well, good-bye whoever you are!"

Several years ago I *remembered* having a strange dream about Patricia. At first I thought I was being shown her child. Then I realized that I was seeing her as an infant. A couple of weeks after the dream, I visited her office and noticed a picture of an infant on the wall. I asked her if it had always been there. In turn, she asked me if I liked it. She went on to tell me that she had just completed a pictorial collage of her childhood. A photograph of her, in infancy, was placed in the center.

As I walked away, I had the feeling that our visit had

been more for her, than for me. At one point during our session, she took a deep breath and stared into my eyes. In a shocked tone, she said, "Maybe that's what happened to me?" In spite of her reaction, I left her office with a deeper sense of myself.

Each passing day the link between myself and my *friends* became more profound. Allowing myself the latitude to confirm my personal understanding, I attempted to reconcile these events with the world I was born. Since there was little in my Western upbringing to help me deal with what was happening, I fell easily into the knowledge I attained from the East Indian Rishi and the Tibetan Lamas, I had studied with in my past.

As time went on, a deepening inner strength led me to intense feelings of knowing. A sense of understanding, stability, and self-sufficiency replaced any doubts I had about my sanity. I thought about the Rishi, I had studied with in my twenties, and all the unusual experiences I shared with him. He had told me they were normal, human experiences. Now I *saw* that those experiences were linked to my *friends*. It was clear to me that he had known!

In spite of the disparity in my experience of the world and what my society *taught*, I was at home in these new clothes. My life appeared as a gigantic jigsaw puzzle with the last pieces moving into place. Moment by moment, my *remembering* became clearer and clearer. What I couldn't *remember* didn't seem to matter. I knew I would know what I needed, when it was time.

I saw other people's lives in a new light. Realizing they could change their circumstances, it became impossible for me to listen to people who repeatedly lamented about their unhappy circumstances. I felt too much joy!

Wholly aware that we are here to live out whatever dream we've chosen, I felt a sense of freedom for myself, and for others. These *realizations* created an immense regard for humanity and all creation. *I saw that we are all* creating and maintaining vast worlds through our perception. *We are all incredibly powerful beings.* Ecstatic with my new found vision, I felt a sense of solace and joy in the freedom it provided. Compassion took on new meaning. Feeling no more sorrow for people's chosen forms of suffering, I was left to feel compassion for those who couldn't *remember* they chose it.

Later that same week Maggie called. She had spoken to a well-established research psychologist about our conversation. As his travel agent and friend, they chatted while she booked him a flight.

He told her he was interested in attending a seminar that was being presented by the Intruders Foundation. Budd Hopkins, a well-known UFO and *Alien Abduction* researcher, had established the Intruders Foundation to unite people experiencing this phenomenon and those who were interested. Her client had originally become interested in this phenomenon after reading a fascinating book by Jacques Vallee, a well-known French scientist and UFO researcher.

Delighted with herself, Maggie believed destiny had opened a door between her two friends. So did I. Without using my name, she quickly shared my experiences. He offered to speak with me. I was delighted there was someone out there I could actually talk to. I called.

When I finally got through to Donald MacGregor, Ph.D., he introduced himself over the phone. Telling me he was not a clinical psychologist, but familiar with the field, he would be happy to talk with me. Providing me an important opportunity, I believed Don was someone I could actually talk to, who was credible. Someone who had knowledge of the *Alien Abduction* phenomenon. While open to the possibility of UFOs and *Alien Abductions*, Don never stated belief. That was fine with me!

Maggie and I were preparing to leave for Italy in less than two weeks. Moved by the prospect of another encounter like the one in Sisters, I wanted to see him immediately, before our departure. Don and I planned a meeting.

The morning of the meeting, I felt some apprehension about revealing my experiences to another psychologist. But the beauty of the day softened my mood. The sun had made an appearance and its warmth had melted away some of the snow. Still, it was very cold. I bundled up for my trip into town.

When I knocked on Don's office door, I heard a voice calling out to me, to come in. Opening the door, I saw a man about four feet away. For a moment I wondered if he was Don. Then I wondered if he thought I was crazy!

A handsome man about my age, Don had slightly graying, strawberry blonde hair, a full beard, and intensely blue eyes. As he looked at me, I had the distinct feeling that he was pleased I looked normal. Then walking toward me, he smiled while extending his hand, and introduced himself. Shaking my hand, he ushered me into his office.

Specializing in cultural perceptions, Don was a consultant to international businesses throughout the world, instructing people of differing social environments on how to perceive and understand each other across cultural boundaries. His credits were as impressive as he was kind.

Don talked briefly about his work, which was very interesting. But I quickly diverted our conversation to

Alien Abductions. Listening carefully to everything he said, I allowed him to share what he knew. He asked me questions about my childhood, affirming the other memories I had already associated with my *friends.* He'd also heard that other people experienced word phrases like, *"It's time to remember."* I was stunned. I hadn't read any accounts of this in the literature.

We discussed other characteristics such as: missing time, certain dream sequences, scars, and other anomalies. Genuine relief replaced my anxiety as I listened to a socially accepted authority talk about these experiences, in person. Meeting only a few times, it was wonderful to talk with Don. He assured me, I was mentally stable. Still these meetings accentuated the fact that I was the one with the answers.

Many people who look to clinical support after experiencing an *Alien Abduction* can easily be diagnosed with Schizophrenia, Bipolar Disorder (the manic phase), and/or neurosis associated with Post Traumatic Stress Disorder. Having studied abnormal psychology myself, I knew my experiences didn't fit into any categories of mental illness. Fortunately there is a growing body of literature, through the work of established and well-respected researchers, which supports the conclusion that people who have these experiences *are not crazy.*

There was one close friend with whom I had been reticent about sharing my experiences. Ruth Adams and her husband were recent transplants from Southern California. Ruth and I had become fast friends when they moved into the house next door. Sharing similar social views, we both appreciated each other's qualities.

Getting together about once a month, we generally had breakfast at a lovely restaurant on the Willamette River, which flows through the center of Eugene. Together, we enjoyed watching the transient beauty of the river flowing beside us as we shared the intimate details of our lives. I delighted in looking into her deep, brilliant blue eyes, listening as she told me stories about how her family fled Poland before the Nazi invasion. She came to the United States with her mother as a young girl, unable to speak English.

Ruth understood that *reality was relative.* Maybe her outlook was due to her extensive travel and unique experiences as a young girl, or maybe it was through an *innate knowing.* In whatever way she had acquired an open and inquiring mind, Ruth had also developed profound inner perceptions.

She was a counselor who had recently retired from a position in charge of assessing the developmental needs of children, with a small, private clinical practice. Since we already shared an intimate friendship, I knew that if I kept my *dream* from her, she would sense my restraint.

Initially, Ruth felt that I may have experienced a traumatic event as a child. I knew that would be her response. After all, it was mine! As time went on, she accepted that this was a real experience for me. Ruth expressed the opinion simply, "There are things we do not know and things we do not understand."

In many parts of the world, UFOs are an everyday part of life. Yet for us, it is difficult to accept things that can't be easily explained. Those who are willing to reveal their experiences are often ridiculed. So their anxiety is reasonable, especially when you consider that even professionals, trained to help people accept themselves, find it difficult to accept this phenomenon. These experiences exist beyond our intellect. To truly assess what *is* or *is not*, we need to open ourselves to the **unknown**, to go beyond **our belief.**

CHAPTER SIX:

VENICE, ITALY

*"The most incomprehensible thing about
the world is that it is comprehensible."
Einstein, quoted
in his obituary
April 19, 1955.*

Although elated about my trip to Italy, I left for the airport that morning with some apprehension. Thoughts of another encounter like the one in Sisters were unsettling. It seemed too coincidental that Maggie and I had planned this trip just weeks before my *friends* had told me, *"It's time to remember."* Still, having lived and traveled through much of Italy, I felt a familiar sweetness in returning to her magic beauty.

Maggie and I were traveling half way around the world, and everything I saw, smelled, heard, and touched were only shadows. There was *something* else in my mind! An awesome place inside my core looked out into the world through my eyes. Realizing my part in this vast *creation*, I felt that *creation* was taking control. All my sensory perceptions seemed muted. Every action, thought, and personal exchange was only an appearance. What I saw with my eyes was merely a backdrop for some predetermined plan, now unfolding. As my life unraveled before me, I viewed scenes that had already been played out.

Somehow, the established link with my *friends* had created a union between my heart, soul, and body. Now immersed in universal awareness, I experienced creation's absolute perfection. Participating as usual in the activities of my life, nothing had changed, yet everything was different. Although vague about the real purpose for our trip, I knew it was perfect.

Our journey started in the early morning hours of March 4, 1993, only a month after my *dream*. Maggie and I kissed our husbands good-bye at the airport and embarked on a plane to Portland, and on to Chicago. From Chicago we took a long flight over the Atlantic Ocean, arriving in Milan, Italy. We then took a train to Venice. When we arrived in Venice, we had one more leg of our trek to endure before our final destination, the hotel, and a bath. We had to take a vaporetto, or water bus, down through the Grand Canal.

Standing in the station, waiting to board the vaporetto, I realized that we had been en route for over 24 hours. I thought I'd be exhausted. Yet my only signs of fatigue were the crusty feeling on the outer layer of my skin, and the dry cotton sensation in my mouth. I was fine, and so was Maggie. Maybe our anticipation of this mysterious adventure diminished any feelings of weariness?

Intensely curious about my recent experiences, Maggie pressed me at every turn. Talking incessantly, we moved through customs, boarding planes, trains, buses and a boat, without the slightest delay or problem. Maggie's curiosity provided me an excellent opportunity to integrate these experiences. We were the only two people in the world. No one could penetrate our bond.

Venice, an ancient and enchanting city, is literally built on stilts. It stands in a lagoon off the coast of northern Italy, in the Adriatic Sea. A playground for European royalty and celebrities, it is acclaimed for inspiring architecture, breathtaking ambiance, and delectable cuisine. Elegant gondolas and boats meander through the grand and petite canals, gracing the city's door step. Since cars are not allowed in old Venice, it felt like we had stepped back in time, as though we had left civilization.

Boarding the vaporetto, I looked back over my shoulder as we pulled away from the Italian coastline. We squeezed into the small boat with *standing room only*. I clutched my bag with one hand, placing it between my legs at my feet, and balanced myself with the other. There was nothing to hold on to. Packed up against strangers, my movements were hostage. I was forced to look ahead to wherever we were going.

The vaporetto's engine resounded in my ears as I watched smoke intermittently billow out the sides and back, emitting a diesel fuel odor. As the boat swayed back and forth, its engine sputtered down through the Grand Canal. I wondered if we would make it.

Early March, it was bitterly cold. Damp, freezing gusts of wind swept into the city off the Adriatic Sea. Glancing up, I noticed dark clouds covering the city. A freezing wind whipped around my face. Numbed by the cold, the sound of the engine, and my vision quelled by the darkness, I took my first glimpse of Venice.

Throngs of people moved swiftly in unison on and off the vaporetto at each stop, along the banks of the canal.

Impeccably dressed men in fine suits and woolen overcoats stood with solemn expressions reading their papers or just standing. Women dressed in heels and furs held their groceries as they swayed gently back and forth in rhythm with the boat's movements. With the daylight fading away, I assumed they were on their way home. Wondering who these people were and where they were going, I tried not to make eye contact. But watching their every move out of the corner of my eyes, I created elaborate scenarios about their lives.

Our hotel was somewhere near the Piazza San Marco. When we reached that stop, we gently pushed our way to the departure area and were swept along by the crowd, like a tidal wave onto the Riva delgi Schiavoni (Quay of the Slavs). An enchanting promenade filled with hotels and restaurants, it was a walkway on the rim of the harbor. We stood on the edge of the Laguna Veneza, a doorway to the Adriatic Sea.

As the crowd dispersed, we tried to retrieve our land legs and establish our bearings. The facade of the Basilica di San Marco loomed before us. This 900-year-old basilica soared into the sky, looking out into the lagoon. Gazing down the Riva delgi Schiavoni, I noticed the gondolas, boat taxis, and a couple of ferries lining the harbor. In spite of the crowd, Maggie managed to get out her map. We stood there huddled together, searching first the map, and then the street signs for the direction to our hotel.

Stopping a few people, we politely told them the name of our hotel, and asked if they could direct us. Unsuccessful, we walked on toward the Piazza, as though we knew where we were going. After a few more pleas for help, we finally found our hotel.

We checked in, bathed, and changed our clothes.

Contented to be there, we were delighted we'd made it. It was seven o'clock, and we were famished. The Piazza San Marco was just steps away from our hotel and provided an array of restaurants. But feeling adventurous, we were drawn in the other direction.

We wandered through the walkways and over the little bridges that crossed the small canals. There, along one of those little side streets, we found a lovely cafe. After a wonderful dinner, we walked back to the Piazza San Marco. The Piazza was quiet. It felt like we were in a scene from an old romantic movie.

Sitting for a moment, drinking cappuccino, we immersed ourselves in the enchantment of Venice. Staring up at the Basilica di San Marco's ornate facade, we were awed by its' magnificence. Five Romanesque domes provided its umbrella and spired Gothic tabernacles thrust themselves into the dark, night sky. They seemed to be reaching for the heavens.

It was grievously cold, yet the night was clear. The light from the stars and the full moon's brilliance, played against this ancient, monumental arena.

Back in our room, I felt grateful that no significant incidents with my *friends* had occurred. I experienced the usual light inside my head, and the already established impressions from my *friends* as pleasant and comforting. Without fear or anxiety, my mind could pass these perceptions off as entertaining. I didn't have to *believe* they were real.

On our second evening in Venice, the hotel clerk had reserved a table for us at an exceptional restaurant. Bundling ourselves in layers of warm clothes, we left for dinner and found the cafe on a small canal off the Riva delgi Schiavoni, just steps from the harbor. The meal and ambiance were stunning.

Walking back to our hotel along the harbor, we noticed the darkness out over the sea. The light coming from the hotels and restaurants that lined the harbor lit up the walkway. Where they failed, the stars and moon provided a soft illumination.

Two policeman walked toward us. I heard them addressing someone, but I didn't know they were speaking to us. After looking around, I realized we were the only people out there. We smiled and walked on. Slowing their pace, the officers began speaking to us very fast in Italian. We tried to make it clear that we didn't understand them, without really knowing if we were succeeding. Playfully, they amused themselves at our expense. We decided to just smile, laugh, and walk away. I was relieved when they walked on.

As Maggie and I turned away from the officers, I glanced out over the lagoon. There I saw an array of sphere-shaped crafts, like the one I'd seen in Oregon. They hovered above the horizon, over the sea between 50 and 200 feet in the air. Some were close to the harbors edge, while others were far off in the distance.

Instantly a thought caught my mind's attention. Here we were in Venice, and across the Adriatic Sea was Yugoslavia. A country whose heart is torn by a bitter conflict between two cultures. War raged only a few miles away! People were dying. Although my emotions were stirred by these thoughts, I was hurled back into the moment.

Telling Maggie what I had seen, we quickly fled the harbor. Once inside the Piazza, we were protected by the arcade of shops and the massive basilica. We didn't talk about the ships. It didn't seem appropriate. The gravity and magnitude of these experiences could not be conveyed in spoken words. Words only interrupted the experience! Sitting at a small outside cafe, we sipped cappuccino. Quietly we delighted in the expansive canopy of stars and the full moon over our heads, distinguished against the black space of darkness.

The next day, Maggie and I explored gift shops and the famous, outdoor Rialto market. I found an elegant crystal sailboat for Mark, and a lovely moss colored suede jacket for Jennifer. For myself, I found a delicately colored perfume bottle with gold accents. Checking prices carefully, we noticed that the gifts and souvenirs in the shops around the Piazza were twice the price as the same items at the Rialto market. Although I was thrilled with my bargains, what we did in Italy, didn't seem as important as the relationships we shared with the people.

Maggie, an excellent cook, is also a connoisseur of fine cuisine. So when it came to choosing restaurants, she was flawless. Just looking in the window of a restaurant gave her the necessary information to judge whether we'd have an awesome dining experience. Turning her head away and wrinkling up her nose was an indication the food was less than superb. She maintained that standard throughout our journey.

One afternoon, on our way to the Rialto market, Maggie gazed into a few small food stores, searching for that special one. The shops looked like little neighborhood grocery stores. At home, they'd be import shops with very expensive cuisine. But here, the specialty foods were available just for the asking, and with reasonable prices, too. Finally finding the perfect store, we went in. Maggie eyed the specialty foods, picking out those items she had to have and asking the salesperson about items she was looking for.

Entering the shop, I suddenly became nauseous. Making every effort to stay with Maggie, I tried to be attentive. Stubbornly I was unwilling to let myself be drawn into these physical sensations. I attempted to control them. Finally overwhelmed, I excused myself and fled the shop.

Outside I leaned up against a huge stone pillar. Looking up I saw nothing but gray clouds lingering above the tops of the buildings. My legs began to buckle under me. I relied on the pillar, believing it would hold me, and began to lose consciousness. As I leaned into the pillar, I felt my shoulder merging into the stone. The oddest feelings and sensations began taking me over. There was no distinction between where I ended and where the stone pillar began. Looking out into the street, I saw nothing out of the ordinary. But the blue-white radiant light began flooding into the top of my head with great intensity.

Paralyzed, a strange spinning sensation whirled deep within me. For a moment I thought I was experiencing vertigo. I tried to maintain as the swirling continued. Then a chilling gust of wind came up out of nowhere, almost blowing me off my feet. I stood there braced against the pillar just trying to maintain my balance and footing. The light intensified, pouring into my head. Suddenly I realized that light was shooting out my finger tips, my head, and the rest of my body.

Where the streets had been empty, they began to fill with people. Tourists and locals went about their business. They shopped and stood at the bars in the little cafes along the cobblestone street, eating and drinking cappuccino. No one noticed me. It was as if I were invisible.

Shops were filled with the sounds of conversation and laughter. I stood there braced against the stone pillar with the light flowing into me, then flooding out into them. My breath was gone. I was motionless. It seemed to go on forever. Finally, the light gradually dissipated.

Maggie danced out of the shop with her merchandise in hand, beaming. She smiled from ear to ear. Talking a mile a minute, she chattered about her purchases as we walked toward the famous 16th century Rialto Bridge. Near the bridge, we stopped for cappuccino. Sitting at a quaint outdoor cafe we enjoyed the atmosphere around us, and watched the gondolas and vaporettos pass by. I told Maggie what had happened. We both knew there was nothing to say!

We sat on the canal, captivated by the magnificent marble, brick, and white limestone palaces all around us. They were built in the 14th- and 15th-century. Their sea-resistant limestone foundations stand on massive stilts driven deep into the lagoon bed. We were awed at the architectural genius.

Finally strolling back to our hotel, we stopped again to pick up some food and wine. Absolutely all the stores and shops closed at noon and didn't reopen until 4:00 P.M. So, if we dallied, we wouldn't get anything to eat. After picking out some wine, bread, and fruit we returned to our room. There we meditated, napped, ate, and discussed our plans for later that afternoon.

The next afternoon we walked back to our hotel, after a morning of sightseeing, and stopped to pick up some food. Once inside our room we meditated and napped. After awakening Maggie said, "Why did you brush my leg? Did you want to ask me something?" I looked at her, stunned. I was about three feet away and hadn't gone near her. Looking into one another's eyes we knew who it was!

Years ago, the Rishi I had lived with in Indian had

talked about the microcosm being a reflection of the macrocosm; that each of us is an expression of creation, and as that expression, we have the potential to comprehend the universe. He would go on for hours describing in detail how everything within us is an exact reflection of everything outside us. "We are all connected by our very nature."

I had left those precepts behind so many years ago, living out my life as it unfolded. Now everything that I had learned was manifesting, not as an intellectual perception, but as *cognition.*

Looking at people's physical image, I no longer saw just their form. I saw an egg shaped radiant light surrounding them. I was now privy to the private worlds of others through my new awareness. My consciousness floated out from my body, and merged in and out of everything, both animate and inanimate.

The following day the clerk at the hotel arranged for us to go to the Island of Murano. Early that morning we dressed for the cold weather and met an attractive man from the Chamber of Commerce. Chatting along the streets and over the bridges, he escorted us to a boat taxi, which he had hired. Then we embarked and poised our cameras.

As the boat sped away from the dock, huge waves fanned out behind us. The small canals were as smooth as glass, reflecting the sparkling sunlight and the stunning architecture. We glided through the water under the little bridges with the engine roaring and the wind whipping through our hair. Out into the lagoon, we came into a small port at the Island of Murano.

Although we knew the Island of Murano was a tourist-trap, we enjoyed watching a little old man blowing molten globules into a clear glistening, glass giraffe. The manufacture of glass has existed on the Island of Murano since 1292. The furnaces were moved away from Venice's city center because of the hazards.

The next day we toured the Palace del Dulce. A palace for the monarchs of Venice, it housed the artifacts of her antiquity. While we toured the Palace, I noticed the religious art had a repeating theme, illustrations of *rays of light* coming down from the heavens. Filtering through clouds, these *rays of light* fell upon the heads of those depicted as having experienced divine revelations.

After Venice, we went to Milan for a night and then home. By the time we arrived in Milan, I was overjoyed to see a McDonalds. Although I'd never eaten there in the States, I was delighted to see something that reminded me of home. The food in Italy was sumptuous and our trip had been magnificent. But I was ready to go home.

During those days in Italy, it became even more apparent there was nothing more important than loving myself. Grasping this understanding was the critical element to *remembering*. Through the love I experienced for myself, I merged into universal awareness, moving into fathomless inner dimensions and understandings. It was there I embraced that unspeakable place, deep within my soul.

A few months after my return from Venice, Mark and I were on our way to San Francisco on business. We boarded the plane, and once in flight I decided to meditate. I closed my eyes, and in moments I began to feel my *friends* close by. Seated next to the window, I opened my eyes and looked out. I couldn't see anything, but I felt them there with my mind. As I closed my eyes again *they* began to communicate.

I had told my *friends* to withhold any memories or

intrusions into my life that might be upsetting. I didn't want to *remember* anything too terrifying. While I knew making a deal with *them* on a rational level was absurd, it soothed my ego.

Visions started appearing in my mind of the trip to Italy. Maggie and I were in what appeared to be a round room, like in the spherical ships I've described. At first confused by what I was seeing, I realized we were in a large corridor with seating along the smooth, curved walls on both sides of the room.

Maggie was wearing what looked like a hospital dressing gown. She was seated across from me with one leg dangling over the other. Swaying her leg back and forth, she laughed. We were having a great time, laughing at each others ridiculous jokes. Then three other people I knew appeared in the corridor, off in the distance. Interrupted by the flight attendant, my vision ended.

Mark and I took a van limousine to the St. Francis Hotel. When we arrived at this old and beautiful hotel, we checked in and had lunch. The restaurant was on an open mezzanine near the entrance that was flanked by towering fluted marble columns. Mark and I watched people as they came in and out while we ate.

Appreciating our time together, we walked around Union Square. Mark had a full schedule of meetings set up for the following day. I planned to do some reading.

In the morning after Mark left, I went out shopping. Then after walking back to the hotel for lunch, I returned to my room. Reading for a while, I suddenly became sleepy. As I lay down and closed my eyes, I began seeing the same scenes that occurred on the airplane. Now the vision continued.

I saw Maggie and me in a room together. It was a

large corridor with metallic, curved walls. Maggie sat across from me on what looked like a table extending out from the wall. It was a seating area. There was a door on her left. I faced her. We laughed and giggled, exactly as I had envisioned on the plane. Then I realized that I'm wearing the same dressing gown she is. Also there is a door on my right. We are mirrors of each other! Continuing to laugh and talk, I have the feeling we are waiting for something. We are here to carry out a task. We know exactly what we're doing. Unconcerned, everything feels as it should. Everything is in its place.

The room begins to fill with men, women, and children, all walking in a uniform manner. Slowly, with even steps, they move into the room, appearing catatonic. With glazed stares and no facial expressions, they seem to be entranced.

Maggie gets up from her seat without hesitation. She continues laughing with me as if nothing has changed. Her actions are automatic. Rising, I move to the door on my right. Our movements are simultaneous, paralleling each other perfectly. We know exactly what to do. As I'm watching, I realize that it is only now that I have the awareness of who I am.

Then Maggie's focus shifts from our laughter to the task at hand. She opens her door. I open mine. Watching her carefully, I realize her door is a portal into another dimension. There beyond the doorway is a breathtaking landscape. The awesome scene is intensified by the contrasting gray, metallic doorway. My eyes engage my mind in the rich shades of green grass, gently waving across an immense meadow. Rolling hills span out endlessly under a soft, golden sunlight. The grass plays against the hills, rippling in a warm, gentle breeze. This is the place I visited as a child.

The people in the corridor form lines, walking in procession. Guided to us by others I cannot see, Maggie and I fulfill our duties. Each person moves toward us, to the portal that provides entrance into their chosen dimension. Single file, they pass before us. Floating through the portals, they step into their world.

Standing to one side of the door, I watch as Maggie guides each person through her portal. Our minds show them the way. I am suddenly aware! These men, women and children are *dead.*

CHAPTER SEVEN:

FROM THE CENTER OF THE LIGHT

"If you seek the kernel, then you must break the shell. And likewise, if you would know the reality of Nature, you must destroy the appearance, and the farther you go beyond the appearance, the nearer you will be to the essence."
Meister Eckhart

After my trip to Italy, I felt I needed to delve deeper into my memories. My *friends* had opened a door, telling me **"It's time to remember."** They laid me bare to an astonishing terrain of fathomless inner dimensions. I needed to fuse these realms into my conscious understanding.

Research provided information, but no answers. There were no directions on how to live in suburban America while these extraordinary events took place. Since I had clear memories of incidents that I knew were associated with my *friends,* all I wanted was a stage to expand my *remembering.*

Hypnosis was widely used by respected professionals in *Alien Abduction* cases. Still I was skeptical about its practical value. Secretly, I had always believed that people fabricated their experiences while under hypnosis, at least to some extent. Of course I hadn't *believed* in UFOs until January 31st, 1993, either. So it seemed ridiculous at this point to argue with myself about whether or not I should try it.

It was nearly impossible to find a therapist who was open enough to talk to me. When I told them *why* I was interested in being hypnotized, they couldn't wait to get off the phone. Eventually one clinician who returned my call with a trembling voice, referred me to a psychologist who I will refer to as Dr. Karin Butler.

An attractive, fragile-looking woman, Karin had blonde hair and green eyes. She and her husband had moved to the Eugene area from Southern California, purchasing a ten-acre parcel of land, just outside of town. When I called Karin, she told me that one of her friends had had similar experiences. While she had never worked professionally with a person who experienced *Alien Abductions,* she was open.

Karin shared some personal experiences with me, showing her respect and sincere interest in unusual phenomena. One summer evening, shortly after moving to Oregon, she and her husband were sitting on their porch, enjoying the night sky. Suddenly they saw what they believed was a UFO. Watching it closely for several minutes, Karin told me how it quickly changed directions, several times. Neither she nor her husband believed that it was possible for conventional aircraft to accomplish those kinds of maneuvers.

I had become acutely aware that whatever relationships I shared with others took place in a dynamic exchange of energy. It was critical for me to be myself in every situation. All the people I associated with, on any level, including myself, were absolutely perfect. These experiences were not just for me. They were an opportunity for Karin to explore those aspects within herself. Instead of accepting a role as her client, or as a victim, we looked into these wondrous events together.

My first meeting with Karin was on the 24th of March. It was at this time that I fully shared the details of my *dream* and the other unusual experiences that had occurred throughout my life. Karin seemed confident that I had *remembered* these events accurately. She wanted to use our time to look at the other incidents that she felt were related. Still, I wanted to look at my *dream* under hypnosis.

In spite of my remarkable recall of the events on January 31st, I wanted confirmation. I thought if I could just talk freely about these experiences, maybe they would seep into all the layers of my mind. Hypnosis was a way to look at them from another perspective.

Our first session was on March 29th. But having never used hypnosis before, I was nervous. Karin eased my fear, telling me that hypnosis wouldn't reveal anything I wasn't ready to *remember.* So with my rational mind consoled, we began.

Closing my eyes, I relaxed as Karin began putting me into a trance. It took about fifteen minutes. I was astonished. Hypnosis was similar to relaxation techniques I had used in the past. My mind didn't go anywhere!

While I didn't *think* I had any conceptions about hypnosis, I did. I thought I would lose awareness. Instead, my conscious mind took a break while Karin asked questions of my subconscious mind and body. Recounting the events of January 31st, they were exactly the same. But under hypnosis, I remembered more detail.

By our next meeting on April 12th, I knew what to expect. Karin suggested we focus on an event that took place when I was twenty. Having briefly told her about this incident in our first meeting, she felt it would be a good place to start.

The incident had occurred in the fall of 1969, but it had really started in the mid-summer of that year. My girlfriend Mary had talked me into going to a lecture on meditation.

One evening after work, Mary dropped by my house with a picture of this odd looking East Indian man. She thought that I might want to go to a lecture on meditation. I remember looking at the photograph and thinking, what a strange looking person. Unfamiliar with what meditation was, I wondered why she thought I'd be interested. Mary begged and pleaded, assuring me it would be fun. Although unconvinced, I agreed to go.

The following Wednesday, Mary picked me up from work. It was a warm, summer evening and we headed for the University of Washington in her 1965 red mustang convertible. With the top down we prattled away about political issues while the Rolling Stones blared out from the radio and the wind fluttered around our hair.

Mary and I had known each other since the seventh grade. Always very popular, she was a petite, beautiful young woman with green eyes and long, straight blonde hair. Mary's young life had been plagued with tragedies. But she had survived them well. Like many of us, she didn't know what an amazing person she was. I loved her.

Late for the lecture, we frantically searched for a parking spot. We drove repeatedly around several blocks. Finally we found a place. Then we had to dash across the huge campus to the building. Fortunately we knew where we were going.

Opening the closed door to the lecture hall, we sheepishly edged our way into the room without looking at the speakers. Breathless, we were both panting. Still we tried to be as quiet as possible. Working our way through the filled rows of seats to the back, we found two empty chairs. I scanned the room as I put my purse on the floor next to my feet, hoping we hadn't disrupted the lecture.

A man walked back and forth in front of the classroom. Occasionally drawing on the chalk board, he talked about the purpose of meditation in today's fast paced life. Astonished, I saw sitting at a table, facing the audience next to him, my eighth grade Social Studies teacher, Mrs. McGowen! My surprise was even more profound because we had shared a deeply personal relationship. Suddenly this lecture was more than a way to reluctantly spend a Wednesday evening. It was credible, worth my attention.

The man speaking finally turned to Mrs. McGowen and introduced her. She was his wife. Mrs. McGowen stood and began addressing the audience. I listened.

The ideas they introduced during that hour and a half made sense. Not only did they discuss philosophical concepts, but they offered a tool to acquire the knowledge ourselves, meditation. Talking about responsibility she said, "If you want to change the world, you have to start with yourself. We influence the universe through our thoughts. Through meditation we clear our minds and bodies of stress. Thereby enabling us to see the world as it was meant to be seen." I was hooked. The following Saturday I started to meditate.

Meditation changed my life. I became more careful about what I ate and found myself embracing other systems of thought. While I had always been interested in other perceptions of reality, meditation was a conscious act, not just talk. After meditating for only a few months, the world around me began to appear different. Colors took on more intensive hues, my hearing increased in acuity, and I experienced immeasurable joy. Seeing the world from fresher eyes like a child, I felt a sense of purpose. I had linked myself to that *something*, the *something* I had so desperately been seeking in my youth.

As a child, I had the feeling I was here to serve some purpose. But I couldn't *remember* what it was. By the time I reached my teens, I was certain I had missed *something*, somewhere. If what I saw was all there was to life, I didn't see the point. If living for food, wealth, status, survival, and a job was all that was happening here, then I didn't want any part of it. I needed to find meaning to life, not other people's meaning, mine.

By the fall I'd become involved with a group who enjoyed meditating together. I was fascinated by what they told me about the East Indian man who had introduced this meditation in the States. Apparently he was a spiritual leader in his own country, a Rishi. It seemed awesome to me that this simple technique could produce such a powerful impact on my life.

After high-school I had gone to a private college for a single term. But feeling indifferent to my studies, I dropped out. At the time, I thought the only real way to experience life was through work and travel. So I took a few classes at a business college and found an excellent job as an executive secretary to the comptroller of a large corporation.

One Friday evening in late September, I left work worn out. Seattle was experiencing its typical fall weather, cold and rainy. After a thirty minute bus ride, I walked up the hill in the dark, to my house. Looking ahead I noticed there were no lights on. I just assumed my roommate hadn't made it home from work yet.

Reaching the door, I put my key in the lock and turned it slowly. As I heard the lock click over, I felt something eerie inside the house. I hesitated at the door.

It was more than the dark that bothered me. It was *something* else. For a moment, I wondered if I should go in. But I was tired, cold, and wet. Therefore, it wasn't worth considering. I went in. Stepping into the dark foyer, I felt a presence. Reluctant to go any further, I stood there assessing my surroundings.

The foyer was about five feet long, six feet wide, and very dark. I couldn't see anything. Removing my wet coat, I reached out to the hall closet. Finding the knob, I opened the door and hung it up. Then slowly moving into the living room, I headed toward the fireplace. The fireplace was on the right, fifteen feet away.

As I moved into the living room, the feeling of a presence permeated the darkness. It emanated out from the far corner, between the window and wall. I tried to ignore it.

The room was cold and dark. I thought if I could work my way over to the brick fireplace without getting hurt, I could start a fire. When I reached the hearth, I fumbled around in the darkness, looking for the box of matches we kept on the mantel. My heart pounded wildly throughout my body and up into my throat. Then it leaped with joy when my hand touched the box of matches.

As my eyes began to focus, I grabbed some newspapers and kindling. Quickly, stuffing them into the fireplace, I clumsily tried to take a match out of the box.

Instead they all fell to the floor. Now on my hands and
knees, I fortunately found one. After a few desperate
strikes, I watched the match ignite. Carefully cupping my
hands around the small flame, I slowly moved the match
under the crumpled paper, praying it would sustain itself
long enough to light.

My fear began to dissipate once the fire began to
crackle. But the feeling that a presence was watching me,
didn't go away. The fire began to flicker throughout the
room, providing a soft warm glow. Afraid to go any further,
I decided to meditate, believing that the presence would
vanish. Settling into a red overstuffed rocking chair, I tried
to relax.

Gazing into the fire, I was drawn into its quivering
flames. Although I was aware of the presence, I shunned
my fear and focused on the white, golds, blues, reds and
yellows, flitting through the blaze. In a blank stare, I
watched the flames weaving in and out. The light danced
on the walls and furnishings throughout the room and I *saw*
everything, yet focused on nothing. Now, even with the
intrusion of that unsolicited presence, I began to entertain
sweet feelings of well-being. I closed my eyes and began to
meditate.

Suddenly my chair began rocking back and forth. My
eyes shot open! The rocking instantly stopped. As I closed
my eyes again, the chair again, began rocking. This time I
kept my eyes closed. Making a conscious effort to stop the
motion, I found I had no control. Someone or *something
else* dominated my body. My mind began to spin in terror.
My eyes shot open!

My body was completely rigid, paralyzed. Then it
began to move. Rising from the chair, I turned and walked
toward my bedroom. One foot in front of the other, I

slowly moved through the living room. My body moved, as if manipulated by strings. Even my breathing seemed out of my control. When I finally reached the bedroom, I lay on top of the bed, straight as a board. The presence was now in the corner of that room.

Trying every mental trick I could think of to pull myself back, I lay there, suspended in time and space for what seemed like eternity. At around 4:00 A.M. in the morning, the presence made itself known.

A blue-white radiant light, began to emerge in the shape of a star. In the corner, where the presence was concentrated, the light expanded out, filling the room. From deep within me and outside me at the same time, I heard the sound of a sweet, male voice. Piercing into my body as I lay paralyzed, the voice and the light carried an infinite love. Speaking in melodious sing-song intonations, while firm and clear, he said, "Joy, give me your heart! Joy, give me your heart! Joy, give me your heart!"

The light floated to the foot of my bed and slowly began to hover above me. A lingering soft, warm blanket of light spread a deep abiding love all over me, merging into the very core of my soul. Flowing up from my toes, over the top of my body, it engulfed me. When the light reached my head, I was released from its paralyzing hold. Before I drifted off into a deep, sweet sleep, I was loved and cherished in a way I had never known before.

When I awoke the following morning, I found myself under the covers with my nightgown on. My body tingled as I *remembered* the previous night. Looking down at my nightgown, I wondered when I had put it on? When did I get under the covers? It was Saturday morning. Thank God I didn't have to get up for work.

The voice echoed through me, and I *remembered*

everything leading up to the moment when the light immersed my soul. *Something* had happened to me. I was changed.

Although exhilarated by the love that emanated from the light, I didn't know what to think. Crawling out of bed, I ran into the bathroom to look at my face. Peering into the mirror, I *saw* that I was different. There in the mirror, looking back at me, was my own likeness. A blue-white radiant light was shooting out from my head. In a purely joyous state, I wondered who that was looking back at me. It was not my face.

Turning around, I heard a key enter the lock at the front door. I came out of the bathroom and stood in the hallway as Janet, my roommate, came in. Stopping in the entry, she saw me and yelled, "What happened to you?" I wondered what she was talking about. Sure, I was standing there with a big grin plastered all over my face. But how could she know something had happened? She said, "There is blue light coming out of your head!"

She told me that she hadn't come home last night because she had heard me talking with someone in my room the night before, late into the night. I had no idea what she was talking about. I had no recollection of talking to anyone, particularly late into the night.

I wandered around Seattle that day trying to figure out how to give my heart, to serve creation? What I didn't understand was that I had already given my heart. It had already happened! I just had to live it out.

Within a few days, I felt an overpowering urgency to travel to India. I sent a letter to the Rishi, sharing the substance of my experiences, asking him if I could come to India to study with him.

Over the next few months, I became aware of three

Beings of light. *They* had been with me that night. Appearing as outlines defined in space, *they* had a white, sparkling light breaking through their periphery. I saw them more as an internal experience, yet their presence was clearly perceptible.

They laughed, joked, and communicated in unison with love and kindness. Although astounded by these apparitions, these three *Beings* brought me incredible love and joy. Creating a profound atmosphere of warmth and peace, I understood that it was their duty and joy, to love and care for me.

Delighting in their presence, I *believed they* were Angels. *Believing* like a child, fully in my heart, *they* had come to guide me. I never again heard the voice, but always felt it's love within me. The three *Beings* of light were not the voice that had spoken to me that night, but their work with me was the same.

As I walked in downtown Seattle during my lunch hour one day, I began to feel as if I was floating. Strolling along, I felt myself floating ten feet off the ground. Yet I knew that my feet were touching the pavement.

During those moments I experienced immense light and heard an awe-inspiring music. It seemed that the wind carried a sweet harmony of strings, wafting the most divine music I have ever heard.

Struck by the beauty and joy of these experiences, I innocently shared them with others. Believing they came because of meditation, I thought everyone who meditated had these experiences. I told Mrs. McGowen, who had instructed me in meditation, assuming she knew all about it. Soon I realized that I was the only one in the group experiencing these apparitions. Perplexed, I had been told that through meditation we become aware of unseen forces, existing all around us.

My Mom was supportive. Living with the responsibility of four children in a traditional 1950's marriage, she was always open to new ways of looking at the world. She had supported me throughout my life, encouraging my interest in spiritual matters. Although conceding she had no clue about what I was experiencing, she loved me. If I wanted to go to India and meditate for the rest of my life, then that was what she wanted for me too.

I arrived in India in early March. The weather was balmy, with sudden downpours of rain. My journey seemed to go on forever. After arriving in New Delhi, I took a train up through the foothills of the Himalayas to a small village where the Rishi lived.

I had no idea how to speak Hindi. I wasn't even aware that I needed to convert my money into rupees. With the help of an older gentleman, I met on the plane, I went through customs. Kindly, he and his family took me to the train station, where I found myself sitting on the hard wooden seat of a train, chugging its way through the hillside toward the Himalayan Mountains.

My insides shook from the jolting motion of the train, as it made its way up through the foothills. Bouncing up then down against the hard wooden seat, my poor behind experienced more pain with each jolt. I gazed out through an open window that had lost its glass several years before, viewing the beautiful rural scenes. Trying to put the pain out of my mind, I watched villagers dressed in white gauze work their fields with water buffalo.

There were so many strange smells, sounds, and visual experiences. "What am I doing here?" I thought to myself. Then an overwhelming feeling of joy and anticipation would grasp me, and I would again immerse myself in my surroundings.

Pulled out of my thoughts, someone was trying to talk to me. Speaking in a language I didn't understand, the woman next to me was muttering something and pointing to a woman scrunched between two women in the seat directly across from me. It seemed strange that I hadn't noticed the Caucasian woman sitting across from me when I boarded the train.

The lady sitting next to me became exasperated and began to shove my arm. Then pointing to this woman she would say something I didn't understand. Finally I made out the word English. It dawned on me, she was trying to tell me that the woman in front of me was English.

I gazed at the Caucasian woman. Her chin was touching her chest and her head bobbed up and down with the movements of the train. I assumed she was sleeping. The woman next to me smiled proudly, pleased that she had gotten through to me. Thanking her for her effort, I smiled and nodded, looking into her eyes. She understood.

Watching the Caucasian woman nodding in front of me, I kept one eye on her and looked out, at the astonishing images with the other. Delighting in the thought that I might be able to speak to someone in English, I looked forward to her awakening. When she appeared to have her eyes open, I asked where she was from. She understood me! Then I asked her where she was going? In a reserved manner she told me she was English and traveling to this small village in the Himalayas. She was going to the same village I was!

Pressing her for more information, I found she was going to see the same man, the Rishi. She had been studying with him for several years. When she realized I was going to the same place, she kindly offered to introduce me to him as soon as we arrived. There was little said between us throughout the rest of the trip. She seemed uninterested in conversation. Although I was excited to meet her, I respected her privacy and followed her lead. It was enough that she was willing to take me to him.

By the time we reached the village, I was exhausted. After ducking the monkeys swinging in the trees overhead, and enduring the long journey, all I wanted to do was lie down somewhere and sleep. But the English woman insisted I follow her. Diplomatically, I thanked her for showing me the way and told her I needed to find my quarters, to sleep. Politely, I asked if she would like to meet me later? Disregarding my words she grabbed my arm, dragging me up a narrow pathway, through some bushes. In minutes we arrived at a white house set in a small clearing. It was nearly dark. She had pulled me all the way.

Irritated, tired, and feeling I'd had quiet enough of this person, I turned to excuse myself. As I looked up, there before me, walking out of the house was a small East Indian man. He was the man I had come so far to see, the Rishi.

White silk robes draped his small dark, skinned body. Stopping on the verandah at the top of some stairs, he looked first at the English woman, then at me. My mind emptied. Unable to speak, think, or move, his gaze bore through me. When I tried to say something, nothing came out of my mouth. I was paralyzed.

Appearing as a star, his body was immersed in a brilliant white light, flooding out into the atmosphere. Within the center of this dazzling explosion was his small form. The light emanated out from his heart. Without a word, he turned and walked back into the house.

The English woman suddenly released her hold on me and walked away. Slowly, confused and bewildered, I trudged down the footpath toward the compound. Somehow I found a person in charge of lodging. He gave me directions to my quarters for the night, and for the long time I would be there.

The next morning I met with the Rishi, and found my voice. Looking down at the ground, I avoided his overwhelming gaze. In that stance I began to tell him about the remarkable things that were happening in my life. Speaking nonstop, I braced myself, fearful that his brilliance would overcome my ability to speak. He interrupted me saying, "Awe! Yes!" Startled, I gazed up into his eyes. Smiling sweetly into mine, he said, "Very Good! Very Good!" Then while patting me on the head, in his sing-song Hindu voice he said, "You think you are here because you want to. You are here because I called. Now go meditate." So I did.

During the next three years I stayed with him meditating and learning what I could. While I understood most of what he said, when I didn't, I listened. He taught me how to hear. Teaching me to instruct others in meditation, he told me to go back to the States and teach. We remained close for the next eight years.

His teachings provided the framework for truly cognizing what my *friends* have now shown me. Since being told *"It's time to remember,"* I have understood that this man *knew* what I have only now *realized.*

Although I experienced and saw many unusual things in India, the Rishi never encouraged me to focus on my experiences. Watching him with others who obsessed about their phenomena, I saw that he quickly changed the subject. Making light of their experiences, he told them that phenomena was not the point. Incessantly he said, *let go*. Nevertheless, there were certain incidents that happened during those years that had a profound affect on me.

One such experience came as a dream, like many had before. In the late afternoon I went back to my room after lunch, to take a nap before the evening lecture. As I lay down on the bed I instantly slipped into another state of consciousness. Although I felt like I was sleeping, I was very much awake. I saw myself in a large round room that looked like a dungeon. Faint rays of light streamed down into the room from above my head. Looking down over my body, I saw that I was filthy. I wore a white smock over a long, dark dress. The walls were built with large, gray chiseled stones. The floor was dirt, covered in straw. A foul odor permeated the atmosphere. For some reason as I looked down at myself, I was surprised that I looked like Joy. My stomach gurgled and I felt an excruciating hunger.

Sitting there in those surroundings on a pile of straw, I heard a harsh scrapping sound at one end of the room. Stone scraped against itself as I watched a huge stone door being pushed open. Two men came toward me. Taking my arms, they pulled me up off the bed of straw and escorted me out of the dungeon. They led me outside, to a large, round plaza, into the light of day.

My eyes stung from the brightness of the sun. The plaza was typical of those that I had seen in small villages and towns throughout Europe. Crowds of people were moving into the square and gathering around the perimeter of the plaza, creating a carnival-like atmosphere.

In the center of the plaza was a round platform, about ten feet in diameter and four feet above ground level. The two men took me to the platform and lay me on the slab. Shackling my wrists and feet with heavy black wrought iron chains and handcuffs, they stretched my arms and legs from my torso, to their breaking point. All of this seemed like I was a participant in a movie. It was as if I was merely an observer. I felt no fear and I felt no pain.

The two men left and returned with a large board. It was the same shape and size of a common door. Placing it on top of me, they covered me. My face was pressed into the board and I felt an intense pressure bearing down on my body. Then I heard a thundering sound, moving over the cobblestone streets, off in the distance. Closer and closer the sound suddenly stopped at my feet. For a moment there was silence.

The men started grunting and groaning as if they were trying to lift something heavy. Suddenly I felt a powerful pressure thrust down on my legs. A huge boulder was moved onto the board, at my feet. As the boulder moved over the board above my legs, I heard my bones crack and pop inside my skin. I felt no pain, but the overwhelming pressure continued to increase, moving up my legs. I heard the crowd cheering, seemingly off in the distance, as if muffled by the board.

Realizing what was happening, I thought it should hurt. I cried out, more in fear, than in pain. The pressure, bearing down on my body grew as the boulder moved up my legs. Then it stopped at my thighs.

Again there was silence. And again I heard a thundering sound, louder and louder, coming closer and closer. I could hear the heavy breathing and groaning of men as they moved another boulder onto the platform, then onto the board. The pressure now converged on my pelvis as the boulder's force pressed against the board.

A loud crackling sound rang out from deep within me. As they moved the boulder up the board a shuddering thunder rolled out from the very center of my being. A fiery bolt of lightning raced up my spine. From the small of my back it shot out through my entire body, then out the top of my head. A white luminescent form suddenly was severed from my body. It was me! I was dead!

Floating above my body I watched myself lying on the bed. Wrapped in a flowing garment of light, I began walking with the board on my back. I saw myself wandering through the halls of the building, crying. Moving in white clouds of light, I knocked on each door. Patiently, I waited for the soul of the person inhabiting that room to answer. When their *light body* opened the door, I would ask, "Why did you kill me?" As suddenly as I found myself outside my body, I found myself back inside, awakening with a start.

Later, when I returned to the States, I learned that during medieval times in Europe, they crushed witches to death with boulders instead of burning them at the stake.

There were many other experiences during those years in India. I remember awakening one morning to a particularly sweet odor permeating my room. Upon opening my eyes, I saw a Golden Being standing at the foot of my bed. Eight feet tall and four feet wide, his sparkling golden radiance emanated out, filling my room. I was soothed and warmed by his presence.

After I left India I went on to Europe. I stayed in a little town in the Italian Alps. One afternoon I was standing on the roof of the hotel where I was staying. Often I would go up there to relax and look out over the beautiful lush green valley. I enjoyed watching the sheep herders move their flocks from the hills at dusk, down to the lower meadows for the night. Looking out over a breathtaking valley, I thought about the incredible beauty of creation. As the thought formed within my mind a gust of wind came up, as if to cherish me. Merging into and through every particle of my body the wind literally took my breath away. For a fleeting moment, we were *One*.

Often throughout my life a *sense of knowing* came to me through the wind. *It is only now* that I *see* how all these events are related. I understand that all these events are linked to my *friends*.

With all these memories clear in my mind, Karin and I had our second session on April 29th. I was ready to *remember*. We focused on that night in the fall of 1969, when the light came out of the darkness and asked for my heart. Karin believed that the light flowing over my body was a screen memory. One that she felt was designed to be uncovered.

Putting me into hypnosis, Karin took me back to the moment I walked into the house on that dark, rainy night in Seattle. The incident began as I previously described. But what I had not remembered was unthinkable. In the living room, when I was stunned into paralysis, there were four *Beings* dressed in dark blue body suits, standing in the corner of the room. Following me into the bedroom, *they* stood in the corner, hidden by the darkness.

A luminescent blue-white light appeared, and out of the light the sound of a male voice merged into me, asking for my heart. Moving toward me as I lay on the bed, the light engulfed me and I floated into a beam of blue-white light with the four other *Beings*.

I found myself walking along a corridor. From out of nowhere, I looked down and realized that the *doctor* was holding my left hand. As I walked into the examining room, the *female* *Being* welcomed my arrival. Her warmth and love rushed to greet me. Taking off my clothes, I lay on the table. A huge, metallic-looking machine emanated light into me while it was passed over the top of my body. As the light flowed over me, I knew that it was checking my body for disease.

A fire inside my head radiated out into the atmosphere. I was happy to be there, at one with my *friends.* Nothing seemed out of the ordinary. I had done this *many* times before. The *doctor* appeared at my feet and began working on my body. Joking, I told him I was going to do to him what he was doing to me. Part of his work was gynecological. He laughed. We both knew that was impossible. Still, he appreciated my humor. Powerful feelings of love flowed back and forth between us.

After *they* completed their work on my body, I was dressed in my nightgown. *They* had brought it from my bedroom. Now *they* led me to another part of the ship, and I was seated on half of a seat, off to one side of a dimly lit room. My legs aligned themselves with the legs of the chair. The *doctor* came into the room, and putting an instrument up through my vagina, into my uterus, he removed a fetus.

The light continued to emanate with a fiery intensity from the center of my head. I felt no pain, no discomfort. I knew that the child I had participated in creating was safe. These procedures had occurred before. There was no need to feel any loss or mourning. Everything was as it should be. I felt a tremendous sense of ecstasy, privileged to maintain and nurture a being in my body whose sole purpose was to serve creation, in form.

My *friends* told me that we manufactured and genetically altered bodies in order to enable enlightened

Beings to enter different dimensions of form in the phenomenal worlds. I *understood* my body was a tool, a vehicle, an instrument. It is not *who* I am. My body, like others here on Earth, was created as an expression of creation for *this* dimension. This was not the only dimension. These were not the only forms.

After completing these procedures, I was led into another room. There, other people like myself stood in the middle of a small circular room on a platform. Projections of nature were cast onto twelve screens at eye level. The projections were like separate films that surrounded us. We stood there, watching. The scenes moved around us while information was imparted. These scenes were not merely the expression of creation for the purpose of opening our hearts, although they produced that affect. *Something* was to take place at these locations. I was especially touched by one scene.

Before me was a scene of snow-capped mountains. A river carved its way down through its crags and crevices. It rushed over rocks with an intense velocity, creating an effervescent, white foam. Flowing into a fifty-foot waterfall, it dropped into a pool of deep, blue-green water.

There was no sound. Yet within the stillness of my mind, I could hear the river roar as it moved onward, plunging over the cliffs. Spellbound, I watched as the water moved with tremendous force, cascading down the shear cliffs, then crashing into the pool. The water splashed up, spraying out into the atmosphere, transforming itself in each instant until it became a fine mist, merging into the air. As I watched the ethereal-looking waterfall gracefully stream over the cliffs, I felt my link with the Earth.

At first it seemed strange that there weren't any people in these scenes. When I mentioned this to Karin, she asked how it made me feel. I was being reminded that the Earth is a living organism. The Earth is as much a part of me, as I am a part of her. Her life force sustains all life forms, here.

After sometime, we were ushered out. I found myself alone in yet another room. Although I could feel other *Beings* around me, I couldn't see them. There were what appeared to be two large machines on either side of me. I stood in the center of the room, alone. The machines looked like those old gigantic computers of the 1950's and 1960's. They appeared to have huge flood lights attached to their surface. The flood lights were turned on, and directed toward my body. Slowly my body was pelted with light.

Struck over and over with different colored light, I stood there. Each color, blue, red, yellow, and green took its turn. At first, the light merged into my body, like waves of sparkling luminosity. But then the speed in which the light was hitting me began to accelerate. I became lightheaded, then dizzy. Tingling and shaking from the inside out, the light continued to barrage me. Each color blended, one into the other, until there was only white. My body started to come apart.

As I related these events to Karin, she asked me to look down at my arm and tell her what I saw. Willingly I forced my gaze downward toward my arm. There I saw a black space with sparkling flashes of white light. My body had become particles of light that were dispersing, farther and farther apart.

Watching myself expand outward, my molecules merged into, then through, the physical limits of the ship. My head went past and through the roof, on into the space beyond.

Although disoriented, I enjoyed the sensations. Laughing with joy, I felt blissfully happy, exhilarated. But as I expanded out into the universe, I began to feel alarmed. If I continued to disperse out into space, I might not come back.

Keenly aware of how scattered my molecules had become, I began to panic. I told them that I'd gone far enough. It was time to stop. *They* assured me over and over again, "It's okay, you're all right." Still, I thought I was going to disintegrate. Instead of bringing me back, *they* pushed me even further. As fear began to replace my joy, slowly my particles began to merge back together, until I was back to myself.

At the moment my body reached its original configuration, I felt my feet touch the floor. The *Beings* standing near me flung me to the floor, wrapping me in a sheer, translucent fabric. The garment held my molecules in place. I laid there motionless on the floor with the fabric surrounding me, like a moth in a cocoon. Then I was released.

With my mind still spinning, *they* gently escorted me into another room. Sitting me in a chair, they poured a heavy, clear, thick liquid substance into my mouth. It was the consistency of honey, but it wasn't sweet. The *doctor* entered the room and gave me instructions. He said, "The light is within you. You must go to be with the Rishi. Tell him who you are. You won't remember this, but you will remember what is necessary to accomplish your task."

It's now time for me to go, but I don't want to go back. *I'm home.* This is where I want to be, with my *friends.*

Nevertheless, in a flash, I'm in my room. The *doctor* is holding my hand. Together we stand at the foot of my bed. Ushering me to the side, he pulls back the covers with his mind and guides me into bed. The blankets hover over me. Gently stroking my hair one last time he imparted his love for me and said good night. The covers fall around me, embracing my form. Feeling the warm fluid light flowing from the tips of my toes to the top of my head, I feel his love for me. I'm at peace.

CHAPTER EIGHT:

THE ASTONISHING ENCOUNTER OF 1952

"The last function of reason is to recognize that there are an infinity of things which surpass it."
Pascal, Pensees
(1670), 267.

One night when I was a small child, my family and I were coming home from a drive-in movie. We left after the second show and moved slowly through the lines of headlights. Although it was late, I wasn't tired. My mother slumped over in the passenger side of the front seat, asleep, as we drove onto the street toward home. Dad drove in silence. I was three and a half years old.

Suddenly I heard a noise, coming from the floor of the car. It sounded like the grinding of metal on metal, like a wound-up mechanical toy. A shiver ran down my spine and into the pit of my stomach. Leaning over the big seat, I peered down at the floor. Terror swept over me as my eyes saw a fluffy stuffed toy lamb. It wasn't supposed to be there!

The stuffed lamb, a wind-up toy, was eight inches long

and six inches high. I watched it for only a second as it leaned from side to side, slowly grinding its way across the floor. Gasping for breath, I flung myself back, upright. Pulling my tiny legs up onto the seat, I quickly folded them in front of me. Whatever that thing was, I didn't want it to touch me.

Then a feeling of calm came over me. I smiled to myself thinking that someone must be playing a joke on me. Looking over at my Mom, she appeared to be asleep. Still I pushed her, thinking she was pretending. She didn't move. Motionless, she was slumped over. Her head bobbed up and down toward my Dad who was still silently driving. Then I thought that it must be Dad! He must be the one that was playing a prank on me. "After all, the toy lamb did appear from behind his seat." But when I looked at him, he was preoccupied with driving.

While these thoughts raced through my mind, I kept hearing that haunting, abrasive noise. I wondered where that toy lamb had come from and *who* had wound it up. I knew it wasn't mine!

Lights from the oncoming automobiles flickered through the car, dispersing as fast as they appeared. The grinding noise continued. Gaining all the courage I could gather, again I leaned over the seat to take another peek.

For a brief moment, I saw nothing. There was a split second where I felt relieved. But as I slowly looked to the left, I saw the lamb. Terrified I grabbed my stomach and gasped for breath as I again flung myself back in my seat. The lamb had traveled across the floor. Now it was moving behind the corner of my Moms seat, next to the door.

From that moment on, I couldn't remember anything, except waking up the following morning in my bed, at home with my clothes on. All my life, that event had haunted me. I told Karin about this incident in our first meeting, thinking that it may have something to do with my *friends*. We decided to look into it.

Karin and I met again on April 26th. Putting me into hypnosis, she took me back to that summer night in 1952 as we drove home from the drive-in. We left the drive-in exactly as I described. She took me back to the place in time when I first saw the wind-up toy lamb. I remembered a child's terror. As the lamb disappeared around my Mom's seat, a small spherical ship appeared on the left side of the car, emanating a blue-white light. Sitting on the left, behind my Dad, I looked up into the light.

My Dad was now leaning over the steering wheel, looking up through the windshield at the light. The car began to slow. I watched the back of his head as he drove, wondering what he was doing.

The drive-in was near the Seattle airport, so it was reasonable to assume that the light came from a small, low flying plane. However, Dad was driving the car over to the right, off the road. I could hear the gravel under the wheels of the car as we moved onto the soft shoulder. It was completely dark.

At some point we had turned off the main road. There were no lights coming from other cars. We seemed to be in a remote area, surrounded by trees. The car suddenly stopped. As the engine died, Dad slumped into the steering wheel. The blue-white light flooded the car. Someone was talking to me. Not aloud or in words the way I talked to my Mom, but through my mind. "You're Okay. Don't be afraid." In a split second, I was outside the car, standing in the middle of a dark, deserted road. The toy lamb was under my arm. The light was flooding down over my head, engulfing my three-year-old body. As I looked up into the light, I saw my *friends*. A feeling of peace and joy came over me. I was delighted to see them.

As suddenly as I found myself outside the car, I was floating along a corridor inside the ship. Gliding along with my *friends,* I entered the examining room and lay down on the table. My *female friend* held my head, while the *doctor* checked my body and performed his work. From there, I was taken into a small, round room. Five other children were already there, waiting for me. We sat in a circle with our *female friend.* She was our teacher.

Asking each of us questions, she moved around the circle. We were all given a turn. When she came to me, she asked how I was doing with my family. I told her that my Mom wasn't staying in her body. Therefore, it was difficult for me to fulfill my task.

I understood that my task with my Mom was to help her *feel*. In order to achieve that aim my Mom had to live in this dimension. She had to accept the life she was born into and the limits of the phenomenal world. But my Mom had lost both her parents before she was seven and she had become adept at creating her own reality. My *friend* listened carefully with attention and concern, as I shared my dilemma. She encouraged me to continue my work.

After we completed that phase of our meeting, a new boy was ushered into the group. The *doctor* introduced him as Andrew. He was an African American, about three-years old. We were delighted to have him.

After Andrew's indoctrination, we were told to go play with the other children, "like us." We all knew where to go! Laughing and squealing, we ran through an open doorway. There we found ourselves surrounded by a lavish, green meadow covered in tall softly waving grass. Meeting with the "other children," we laughed, played hide-and-seek, and enjoyed each others company. After a while, the *doctor* came to get me. I thought it was time to go back to my family. But with his mind the *doctor* told me that we had somewhere else to go. We had an appointment.

The *doctor* led me to the control center of the ship, where we stood together, holding hands and looking out over the city of Seattle. The rounded windows captured a spectacular view of the illuminated buildings as they stood tall against the dark cloudy sky, off in the distance.

Slowly the ship turned toward the East. I watched in delight as we sped toward Mt. Rainier. Gliding over the snow-capped peak, we hovered over her Eastern slope. Colossal black and gray billowy clouds leisurely gave way, exposing an enormous ship, suspended in a chasm. Lit up like a Christmas tree, it's multi-colored lights defined it's many levels, unveiling its toy-top shape.

On our approach, I saw that our ship became smaller and smaller. Finally we entered into a huge bay on the lower level of the now enormous installation. It was easily a small city.

Leaving our small ship, my *female friend* took my hand. She led me toward a clear, tubular structure attached to the outer surface of the huge ship. Then standing in front of a clear, glass-looking door that led directly into the tube, we entered when it opened. There was no platform. We stood suspended on air as the door closed behind us. Gently we were swept along by a soothing wind, up to another level.

Reaching our destination, we left the tube and moved into a large corridor lined with smooth, curved walls. We walked briskly, past many different types of entities. They were not human beings as I know them. They were highly intelligent beings, all shapes and sizes.

As we walked along the corridor, a woman stopped us. Leaning down, she looked tenderly into my eyes. Her hand reached out to me. Softly touching my hair, mind to mind she said, "Your hair is beautiful." I felt cherished and loved. This was my world!

My *female friend* and I marched to the end of the corridor and turned into a room on the right. Once inside the circular room, I was seated on a chair in the center. I was to sit there. My *female friend* left the room. Looking over my shoulder I watched as the door closed behind her. Then I heard a sound above my head.

Looking up, I saw a clear, circular glass-type tube moving down over the chair. It encompassed my body. When the tube met the floor, a warm, sweet wind began sweeping around and then into me. Suddenly the molecules that formed my body started dispersing. Slowly, my body began to disintegrate into minute particles of sparkling light. The particles floated to the top of the tube, near its ceiling. The knowledge of who I was before I was Joy was suddenly unveiled. It had always been there, within me.

I *remembered* living on other planets and knew I was from a solar system far, far away. After my *remembering* had completely gathered itself into my awareness, my particles began to fuse back together. I synthesized back into the three-year-old body of Joy.

Converging back into my original form, images of my birth to this world were reawakened. Standing with my *friends,* the *doctor* and *female Being* in a sterile room, I watched my Mother in labor. There were nurses and a doctor helping her. In those moments before I was born, we completed our covenant. I agreed to work in this dimension through a body that *we designed and created.* My form, the time and place of my birth were critical factors in the balance, interplay of creation. I experienced the full knowledge of all the forms of life I had previously taken and all those forms I would take in the future.

At the time of my creation, I was placed in a vessel on a ship whose function was to maintain and sustain forms of life for this dimension. Previously in light form, I was not in this new body full time until it took breath from this world. However, I entered the form from time to time to familiarize myself with its operation. When I did, I felt the buoyant fluid embrace the surface skin and experienced the boundaries of its perceptions.

The clear, glass-like tube slowly lifted. At that precise moment, I was completely synthesized into my present configuration. My *female friend* appeared next to me and together we left the room. *I knew who I was, and where we were going.*

We walked toward another part of the ship in silence. Entering into another tubular structure, we flowed toward an upper level and entered a chamber.

In the center of the chamber was a large rectangular table. Six *Beings* of light were seated on one side. Exuding benevolence, warmth, and love, their forms appeared as an iridescent, golden-white light. Their contours were eight feet tall and four feet wide. Their particles could not be defined as three-dimensional.

Six entities, including myself, sat directly opposite the *Beings* of light. Each was from a different star system. The female being at the end of the table looked similar to our human forms, although her head was larger and she had no hair. The male being next to her had a scaly reptilian appearance. Next to him was a huge being with a beastly-looking hairy form. At the head of the table sat the *Old One.* With the exception of the *Old One,* each had come to this meeting in an effort to preserve their world.

The *Old One* had always been here. He had come long before there was life on Earth. He would be here long after it was gone.

When I entered the room, I observed a man sitting on the right of my designated position, at the end of the table. As I seated myself, I examined his demeanor. Sitting directly across from the *Old One,* he was dressed in fatigues. He was angry. Ranting and raving about being kidnapped, he wouldn't hear anyone. Threatening us, he yelled, "If you don't want the United States government firing on your ships, you'd better let me go." Without allowing any of us to intercede, he rambled on. "I must be dreaming. This can't be real. This can't be happening." We referred to him as the General.

I looked into his eyes, commanding him to "shut up." He looked back at me, stunned. All he saw was the three-year-old body of a little girl. He couldn't see beyond the form. Flabbergasted, he relinquished his power. Then I asked the others what they had hoped to accomplish by bringing him to the table.

For the next few hours we examined ways to intervene in this man's scheme. Involved in military maneuvers, his actions cultivated a climate of violence in an already impoverished part of the world. His fearful and negative rendering of life had the potential to destroy thousands of lives. It was our hope to avert that atrocity, to allay the senseless loss of life. Together we tried to reach him.

Finally I became impatient and told the *Old One* that we were wasting our time. I ordered the others standing around the walls of the chamber to take him back to where *they* had found him.

The General did not understand we were all *One*. We were not the enemy. The impact of his actions would be as devastating to him, as to those he thought, he was damaging. The violence he incited had far-reaching consequences, affecting worlds he knew nothing about.

Our session came to an end when Karin asked me to go back to the car. I said, "No." At first she was agitated and told me I had to go home now. I told her I didn't go back to the car. Surprised, she asked me where I was taken. *They* took me to my house and placed me in my room. I remembered standing in front of my bed with my clothes on and the toy lamb under my arm. Daylight was breaking.

Karin questioned me further. "You mean you went straight home? Didn't your parents miss you?" I said, "I don't know." That was all I remembered.

When I came out of hypnosis, I felt angry. I looked into Karin's eyes and said, "Do you believe this?" My mind could not grasp what I *remembered*. These memories were too much. But the feelings that came with them could not be explained away. The visions and *rememberings* were crystal clear.

Many memories came to me instantaneously during the contact with my *friends*, on January 31st. My *remembering* literally opened up. At the time these strange incidents happened, I didn't understand where they fit in my life. For instance, coming home from school in September of 1958, my best friend's Mom and Dad were all excited. They had seen a spaceship hovering over a telephone pole near our house.

I have clear recall of being with my *friends* on the deck outside my bedroom in Seattle at age eleven. *They* took me for a ride on one of the smaller ships and taught me how to drive it. I sat directly in front of the controls and without touch, the ship responded to my mental images, my commands. At the moment I conceived a thought, the ship reacted. At first it was difficult to get used to and I zigged-zagged all over the sky. But with their patient and kind attention, *they* helped me focus my mind. Within a short time I was in control and having the time of my life.

On November 21, 1963, I went to bed as usual, but couldn't sleep. I lay awake in my bed until I couldn't stand it anymore. I got out of bed and looked out my bedroom window. It felt as though I were waiting for something to happen!

We lived on a hill above Lake Washington. As a child and young woman, I spent hours looking out over the lake, savoring it's soothing, tranquil beauty. On that night the light from the moon shown down on the dark, choppy water. I could hear the small, dark waves forcing their way to the shore.

For some reason I was agitated. Unable to sleep I kept thinking that something was going to happen. I was very upset and felt that whatever was going to happen would affect the whole world. Although I didn't know exactly what it was, I knew it would be devastating. It would affect the course of history.

Finally in the early morning hours I drifted off to sleep. Within those few hours of sleep, I had a dream that someone was shot. Although it was disturbing I awoke the next morning just in time to get ready for school. I didn't have a chance to think about it.

Surprisingly, I made it to school on time. I was sitting in my third period class, when suddenly a boy burst into the class room yelling. Out of breath and sputtering, his words were unintelligible. Finally, I understood what he was saying, "The President has been shot!" Looking into my teacher's eyes, I began to cry.

Mr. Cole, my algebra teacher, was a sweet man in his mid-thirties. He had thinning, light brown hair and wore wire rimmed glasses. He looked like Mr. Peepers. A scientific nerd-type man who hosted a science show on TV in the 1950's. Raising his hands to be heard, he tried to calm the class. Instead, the class broke out in pandemonium. Kids began throwing pieces of paper and pencils at the boy who had burst into the room, yelling at him to quit clowning around.

Mr. Cole left the room and returned a few minutes later. He stood in front of us without a word. Tears trickled from his eyes, under his glasses and down over his checks, to his chin. Slowly the class became silent. Looking out over his class he barely held himself together. He forced himself to speak. With a shaken, weak, but firm voice, he said, "President John F. Kennedy has been shot."

Later, as a junior in high-school, I had another compelling dream. Returning home from school one afternoon, I was extremely tired. So, I lay down to rest. Instantly I fell into a deep sleep, and began dreaming. I was in a small room with no windows. Everything was gray, sterile, and muted.

As the dream unfolded, I realized there was a simple-looking woman beside me. She was helping me dress. Looking down at myself, I realized the clothes were from another era. Gathering up the full dress she reached above me and brought it down over my head. The dress was long, black and fitted at the waist, with long tight fitting sleeves. Several buttons were slowly being fastened up the front of the dress, to the top of my neck, at my chin. The woman, although unsmiling, felt kind. When I finished dressing she escorted me down a long corridor, out an immense stone building and down a flight of steps to the street. At the curb of a cobblestone street, was a black horse drawn carriage.

Gently taking my arm, the woman helped me into the carriage, guiding my foot to the step. Then she sat beside me inside the carriage, and it began to move. I could smell the horses and hear their hooves, clearly strike the cobblestone street. As we hit the uneven stones beneath the wooden wheels, I was tossed about the cab.

Driving through the village, we rode into the country. The carriage climbed a small hill and stopped. At the top of the hill, overlooking a beautiful green valley, stood a huge gray, stone mansion. It was my house!

Opening the carriage door, the woman escorted me out and up the steps of the house. The steps were flanked by two thirty foot stone columns. They provided an entrance to an immense double door. Stepping into a foyer, I looked to my left where two doors were opened to an expansive room with tall ceilings. A stone fireplace took up the better part of one wall. The room was cold, gray and sterile. As the woman led me into the room I saw David standing next to a window. David was my boyfriend. Enraged, his eyes pierced into mine.

At the time I was dating a young man who had grown up not far from my home. David was three years older than I, and a student at the University of Washington. We had been seeing each other on and off for a couple of years.

A servant entered the room with a small bundle and crossing in front of me, placed it in David's arms. Glaring into my eyes, he told me that he wanted to make sure I saw my child. "So you may know what evil you have done. I never want you to forget what you have lost. You will never see your son, again." I began to cry. At that moment I *remembered.*

During the dream I *remembered* I was Joy. Yet in the dream, I realized that David was my husband in another time. He was a successful merchant, several years older than I. Our marriage had been arranged. David went on long business trips, leaving me alone for months. In his absence, I fell in love with a young man in the village and became pregnant.

David continued to look into my eyes with hatred, telling me that he would raise this child as his own. No one would ever know how I betrayed him. The child would never know his mother. To him, I was dead.

The woman at my side grabbed me as I lunged toward my child. Desperately I tried to reach him. The other servants helped restrain me. As they held me back, I screamed and cried, pleading for forgiveness, begging for my child. The woman who escorted me took me back to the carriage, to the cold, stone building. It was an institution, where I lived out my life.

With a start, I awoke. This dream frightened me! It had an indefinable quality that separated it from other dreams. Tremendous emotions gripped me. I mourned the loss of a child.

A couple of hours later, I got an unexpected call from David. He told me that he had applied to Officer Candidate school and was accepted. This was the first I had heard of it. He was leaving immediately. He went on to say that although he loved me, we could never see each other again. Since I was not Jewish, his family forbid him to see me. I never did see him again.

CHAPTER NINE:

THE MESA AND THE EXTRAORDINARY EVENTS MARKING MY ADULTHOOD

"Do not divert your attention to the directing minds of others; look straight ahead to where Nature is leading you, to the nature of the Whole through what befalls you, and your own nature through what you must do, for every man must do what is compatible with his own make-up."

Marcus Aurelius

In the summer of 1972, I left the mystical landscape of India and the tradition of Europe and returned to Seattle. I found a place to live and began teaching meditation. I traveled around the United States establishing centers of meditation, lecturing, teaching meditation, and conducting seminars and retreats. There were moments I longed to go back to India, to the people and places that provided me comfort and knowledge. But I understood that the United States was my home. It was where I belonged.

Soon after my return, I met a handsome young man at the University of Washington. Strangely, Michael and I had met briefly in Athens, Greece, at the outdoor Market.

He had taken a year off his studies and was traveling through Europe. Now we bumped into each other at the University, where he was completing his degree. Michael was from an established, traditional family back East. They were very proper. His father, among other things, was a professor at a prestigious university. Michael was tall and handsome, with black wavy hair and piercing blue eyes. As a child, he was interested in understanding the nature of life. His family had traveled extensively throughout the northern hemisphere, and to exotic places like Indonesia and Malaysia. Consequently, he was open to many different ways of looking at the world. We quickly fell in love.

One morning, in the winter of that same year, I awoke in the early morning darkness. Cushioning my back against the wall, I sat up and closed my eyes to meditate. Instantly, a vision unfolded.

Seven feet in front of me, above my bed, was an explosion of blue-white light. Within the light was an image I recognized as Jesus. Standing on a cloud of white luminosity, he wore a flowing robe of brilliant light, draped around his body. His arms extended out to me, palms exposed. Dazzling rays of blue-white light pierced through the center of each palm, descending into the crown of my head. Experiencing an overwhelming love, I began to cry.

That experience powerfully impacted my heart. The light that came through Jesus into me, was the same blue-white radiant light I experienced with my *friends*. *It was the same light inside me.*

A few months later I began experiencing nausea and flu-like symptoms. Upon visiting my doctor, I found I was pregnant. My due date was calculated for November 10, 1973. Since puberty, I had experienced sporadic menstrual cycles and often went for months without any periods. So, it didn't occur to me I might be pregnant. Still, Michael and I were delighted and were soon married.

The pregnancy seemed to proceed normally, although I was constantly ill during my first trimester. At the end of my third month, I experienced heavy bleeding. Believing I was having a miscarriage, I frantically called my doctor. He told me to go into the emergency room at the hospital. Fortunately everything was all right. But he told me if I were going to keep this baby, I needed to stay in bed as much as possible.

Two months later Michael graduated and landed a teaching position at a private college in Orlando, Florida. Although I slowed down, I continued teaching meditation. It wasn't physically demanding.

During that time in my life, lights were appearing and disappearing. Electrical anomalies with household appliances were the norm. Incessantly, I had the inexplicable feeling that someone was watching me. I tried desperately to overlook any *fearful* feelings I might experience due to my brushes with the **unknown,** because so many of these extraordinary events were profoundly comforting.

On one occasion, I was lying on the sofa and felt someone lay down next to me. At first I thought it was just my imagination. So I ignored it. Then I felt this *Being* turn into light and wrap vast, soft billowy arms around my abdomen, as if to cherish the child within my body.

I had experienced similar feelings throughout my life. There was often an *Angelic Being* of light that came to me. He was different from the three *Beings* that had come that night in Seattle. This *Being* was immense. He would wrap his soft, soothing light around me and lovingly embrace my entire body and soul.

Michael and I were having difficulty adjusting to each other and the pregnancy increased our problems. Being pregnant, I experienced tremendous mood swings that he didn't like! He told me that he was feeling trapped by a wife, with a child on the way. Although I understood how he felt, I had similar feelings. But as a woman, I couldn't just walk away. As time went on, Michael became more and more distant.

My pregnancy seemed to go on forever. After a long and intense labor, our daughter was born on January 8, 1974, two months after her due date. I was so happy, I didn't think about the disparity between her birth date and her due date. She was a perfectly beautiful baby. Still, it seemed strange that a physician could be so far off.

A week and a half after her birth, Jennifer became fretful. I had just taken her to the pediatrician for her first well-baby check-up. Her weight was excellent and her pediatrician assured me she was doing very well.

Michael was busy working at the college, and I was exhausted from the delivery and night-time feedings. Jennifer started whimpering and crying, unlike her normal behavior. I checked her over and over again to make sure every possible problem was taken care of. Then I'd love her, gently rocking her back and forth and talking to her sweetly. I'd lye her up against my breast patting her little back, hoping to release any gas in her stomach. That was all I knew to do. But her eyes looked different. They were glazed.

The evening after these symptoms appeared, I lay her down in her crib, hoping I could catch some sleep for a moment. She continued to cry. I thought, "Oh my sweet baby, please let me sleep." At the moment I laid my head down on the pillow, someone kicked me, hard. Stunned, I looked around the room, but saw no one. Then I pulled myself together, got up, and walked over to Jennifer's crib. Leaning down, I gently felt her head. She was hot. Crazed with fear, I called her pediatrician. He told me to take her to the emergency room and he'd meet us there. Her temperature was 107 degrees.

Frantically, I put in a call to my husband. He was lecturing at the college and had taken the car. Michael left his class as soon as he got my message, arriving at our apartment in minutes. We raced to the hospital.

Jennifer's pediatrician had called ahead alerting the hospital staff we were coming. When we arrived, they took Jennifer directly in for testing. The doctors worked on her, relentlessly throughout the night. Her symptoms were life threatening.

They called in specialists while I anxiously sensed their frustration. They couldn't pinpoint the problem. Performing painful tests on her poor little body, they tested her for everything. Thoughtfully, they allowed me in the room where they performed these tests, to comfort her.

Finally, after all her little veins had been used to draw blood, they told me it would be necessary to go into the veins in her groin. Devastated, I left the room and Michael took over. I waited in the hush of a small waiting area, down the hall from her room. All I could hear were her screams ripping through my body, into my heart.

By the end of the second day they hadn't been able to learn the cause of her symptoms. Jennifer was still in intensive care. Her pediatrician came into the room and pulled up a chair in front of her crib. Gently picking her up, he held her naked, lifeless body in front of him. Her head hung to one side. Gazing into her closed eyes, he looked at her. Then without looking at me, he began speaking to Jennifer. Tears streamed down his cheeks as he pleaded with her to eat, to live.

The next few days and nights I experienced a level of pain I would not have believed possible. Jennifer barely clung to life, while the doctors did everything they could. A cot was brought in, so I could stay next to her. I never left her side. When her temperature soared, I alerted the nurses and helped bathe her in ice. Three days later her temperature broke.

A few weeks after Jennifer was released from the hospital, and her doctor felt she was strong enough to make the trip, I took her to Switzerland. There, we met the Rishi from India. We remained abroad for six months. Staying in the town of Brunnen, our hotel sat on the rim of Lake Lucerne. Our balcony looked off into the Austrian Alps. It was breathtaking. There I found peace, solace and a place to heal from the trauma of Jennifer's near death.

While Jennifer and I were in Switzerland, Michael's contract with the college was completed and his position wasn't renewed for the following year. Without my knowledge, he accepted a position as an assistant manager to a retail chain in Grand Junction, Colorado. When Jennifer and I returned from Switzerland, we moved to Grand Junction.

Maybe it was the stress of Jennifer's illness and my need to care for her, I don't know. But Michael felt his needs weren't being met. Our marriage continued to deteriorate.

In Grand Junction I became friends with the manager of our apartment building. Nadine and I had a lot in common. Although she was born in the mid-west, she was intensely spiritual. We became instant friends.

I liked the idea of raising Jennifer in a small community. But I wasn't accustomed to small town life. Except when living abroad, I had always lived in a city. By the summer of 1975, Michael and I had reached a point where our differences were irreconcilable. We separated, and later divorced.

Nadine was struggling in her marriage, too. We provided enormous support for one another. Nadine had a beautiful daughter named Megan. She was eight.

Michael went home to his family, while Jennifer and I settled into a townhouse and I found a job. Finding adequate child care was a nightmare. But I finally found a good family to care for her while I worked. It was difficult being a single parent. But during my time off, I'd spend as much time as I could with Jennifer. Taking her up to the Grand Mesa National Forest in Western Colorado, near Grand Junction, we would camp out with Nadine and Megan.

Awed by the Colorado landscape, I savored the quiet beauty of the high desert. Seasons changed one into the other and I began to feel a sense of belonging, a feeling of home.

One summer morning, Nadine stopped by my house for coffee on her way to Utah. She had found a new love interest and was on her way to meet him for the week-end.

After she left, I began to feel nauseous. Thinking I was coming down with the flu, I decided to lie down with Jennifer while she napped after lunch. Laying her next to me on my bed, I gently soothed her hair and rubbed her back until she fell asleep. The next thing I remember was waking with a start. It was three days later! Aghast, I couldn't figure out what had happened.

A sharp pain throbbed in my leg. Turning it inward I

noticed a single puncture wound on the outside of my right ankle, near the bone. My entire lower leg, up to my knee, was red and swollen.

I thought I must have been bitten by a spider. What else could have caused me to lose consciousness for three days? What else could have caused a puncture wound and swelling?

Distressed and shaken by this event, I kept thinking I'd been up on the Mesa, back-packing. I must have been bitten by a brown recluse or a black widow spider. Yet, I hadn't been on the Mesa. It had been weeks since we had been camping.

Jennifer was fine. She was clean and satiated. Happily she played next to me on the bed as I awakened. She was only two years old. I couldn't believe I had lost consciousness for that length of time. What if something had happened to Jennifer? Where did I go? Her welfare might have been jeopardized. But nothing had happened. Everything was fine. Jennifer wasn't soiled or crying. She didn't even seem to be hungry. Confused by this bizarre incident, I had to put it out of my mind.

One evening a week later, I left Jennifer with Nadine and drove up into the Mesa. With no idea where I was going, I drove to a secluded area on the plateau. I got out of my car and walked to the middle of a brown, grassy area and lay down. Although shaking with fear, I knew I had to be there. I quickly fell asleep. In the early morning, I awoke cold, in the same place I'd fallen asleep. I had a gnawing feeling there was something else there, a presence. Although I don't remember seeing anything, I thought there was a deer standing over me, looking into my eyes.

There was no way for me to explain these eerie events. Instead, I made every effort to forget them.

Fall came to Colorado and the aspen trees, with their pristine white bark, turned shades of yellow, red and gold. They stood tall against the mountains off in the distance. It was October and Jennifer's first Halloween. Nadine and I had planned to take the girls trick-or-treating together. She lived in a small, suburban community, outside of town.

As Jennifer and I drove to Nadine's, we stopped by the grocery store. At two years old, Jennifer had no idea what Halloween was. But when she realized I was going to buy her a costume, she became very excited. Happily, she picked out a Tweetie Bird outfit and when we got back to the car she wildly unwrapped it. She was ready to put it on. I put it on her over her clothes. With a proud little smile, she was ready.

When Jennifer and I arrived at Nadine's, it was almost dusk. Megan was at the front window, anxiously awaiting our arrival. In a festive mood, Nadine and I made-up Megan and then Jennifer's face. After finishing the last touches, Nadine told Megan, the Queen, to get some grocery bags for their treats. Megan danced off to the kitchen.

Suddenly we heard her screaming. Megan ran crying into the living room in horror. She was out of breath and trying to tell us something. First she tried to tell Nadine. Nadine attempted to understand and calm her, but she was unintelligible. Then Megan looked at me, pleading with her eyes for me to understand. But I couldn't make out what she was saying either.

Finally when she composed herself, she told us that she saw four small people with big heads, no hair, and big eyes trying to come into the back door, through the kitchen. Nadine and I smiled at each other. We assured her that they were just children dressed up in costumes, trick-or-treating.

"They were just trying to scare you," I told her. But Megan could not be dissuaded, or consoled. She knew what she saw, and they were not children.

At the time I was unaware of the UFO phenomenon. So I wasn't able to see the link between this event and the other anomalous phenomenon that had occurred in my life. Nadine and I both appreciated the magical reality of childhood, and believed Megan had seen *something*. But not knowing what it was, we put it aside. It wasn't until my *friends* told me, *"It's time to Remember,"* that I realized this event was related to them.

In September, 1977, I moved to Eugene, Oregon. Having gone through a painful divorce, I was ready to experience something else. I had traveled to Eugene the previous summer, thinking it would be an excellent place to raise Jennifer and start a new life.

The first few months in Eugene were magical. But we were incredibly poor. For Christmas, we spread cookie dough over our huge dinning room table (It was really an old door.) and spent hours decorating cookies. The only gifts Jennifer got that year were from her Grandmother.

In January of 1978, I had an extraordinary dream. On a journey home, I was walking to Seattle from Eugene. Along the way I met a woman, who traveled with me. When we arrived at my childhood home in Seattle, it was being remodeled. It no longer looked or felt like my home. I looked around for a moment, then decided to leave. As I turned to walk away, something pulled me, forcing me to turn around. Then an overpowering impulse drew me through the front door.

When I entered the house, I found myself in a large corridor. Walking along in a trance state, I was drawn in, further and further. Finally I entered a large circular room that felt like a cave. At the end of the room was a presence, an entity. He was not human, but he had form. He was wrinkled and very old. I knew that he was the *Old One*. There were others in the room surrounding him in a circle. There was a place open, waiting for me. I seated myself in the circle.

Once I was in position, an intense telepathic communion began. It came into me from the *Old One,* as he sat at the head of the circle. A symbol of a cross encased in a spiraling circle of light appeared above my head and knowledge from this symbol began to pour into me. The symbol moved down from its place above my head, into my crown, imprinting itself into my head and then down into my body.

The cross represented the two paths of existence in this dimension, positive and negative. Now inside the swirling vortex of light, I experienced them as *One*. They came together in the center. This was not a dream! Knowledge continued to pour into me. As the circular symbol manifested itself inside me, I saw all the levels of creation leading inward to the source. Lines manifesting from the source flowed outward, like rays of the sun, representing the paths of life. This is the *Oneness*. If one *is*, then one exists in *Oneness*.

The next night I had another extraordinary dream. A form in the shape of a diamond was imprinted on my lower forehead, between my eyes. Then a brilliant light poured into me through the diamond. It was like an opening into another world. A brilliant white light streamed in and out of me.

Although these experiences were overwhelming there was no one in my life with whom I could share them. I was forced to keep them to myself.

When Jennifer was ready for pre-school, I went back to school too. Those years were difficult. Trying to be a mother, work full-time, and go the school full-time, was hard. I studied Tai Chi and the healing arts while I continued to teach meditation, when there was time. But my load was overwhelming. For comfort, I kept a journal. Sometimes I wrote down my dreams. Other times, I wrote about my feelings.

One evening after Jennifer had gone to sleep, I crawled into bed. Studying into the night, I finally put my books aside at 3:00 A.M. Although exhausted, I was too wound up to sleep. So I wrote in my journal. Now remembering back on that night, I can feel the intensity of those emotions. Yet I had no memory of writing this passage until the April of 1993.

While preparing dinner, I became aware that I needed to turn the experiences I shared with my *friends* into a book. Suddenly I was struck with an overwhelming urge to go into my office. Once there, I reached up into my bookcase and pulled out a little red book. I thought it was the book that I had used for notes in some special classes. I had completely forgotten that I had two little red books! The book I grabbed was the one I had used to write my feelings and dreams, during that difficult time in my life. It fell open to the passage that follows:

January 28, 1978

Stellular starships coming from distant galaxies have frequented this atmosphere, interceding in the development of our planet.

Please bear with me. Your vocabulary is limited and my structure is vast.

As you pass through other dimensions you will
feel altered states of awareness. This is normal.

Please be calm, relax. Peace is within you.

My presence has been known to you for several
decades.

In this incarnation you are a free-being. Here to
be yourself. You cannot come up with your
origin if you fight your own force. So flow with yourself. Go within and follow the river. Watch it unfold
within you.

You know this is only a way of talking about something that is already formed within you. Your potential is vast. As you now know it, it is demean-
ing and uncomfortable. You are not yet living the
fullness that you are. The magnitude of knowledge
you have at your disposal is incredible and always
available.

Enlightenment is a way of life.

Within the memory of that message, written in my
own handwriting, I *remembered* the powerful feelings of
that night. I had felt as if *something* had interceded in my
life. There was an incredible heat inside my body.

In the early spring of 1979, I saw a poster at the
University of Oregon advertising a lecture on Tibetan
Buddhism. My curiosity was aroused. So I found a baby-

sitter for Jennifer, and went. After the lecture, the speaker, who was a Tibetan Lama, showed us a film. In the film, many Lamas sat in two rows, facing each other. There was one principal Lama in the center, at the top, on a throne. Performing a ritual, the Lamas gave a Tibetan Wong (Initiation). Stunned, I was paralyzed. I *remembered* these ceremonies!

When the lecture was over, I walked to the back of the hall where coffee and doughnuts were offered. My head was spinning as the sounds from the Tibetan ritual instruments vibrated within my bones. I needed to collect myself before driving home. A woman stood next to me as I poured myself some coffee and started talking to me. About my age, with long dark hair, she was very exotic looking. Somehow she had the impression I was involved with a Tibetan Buddhist group. I tried to be cordial.

She told me that she lived in Eastern Oregon, and had been attending a seminar in Portland. The woman began sharing the details of the seminar, as if I knew what she was talking about. Apparently, a celebrated Lama was traveling through Oregon. Suddenly she stopped talking for a moment and looked into my eyes. She said, "Did you say your name was Joy?" I said, "Yes." Then she told me that the Lama in Portland had asked for a person named Joy. I was astounded. Continuing she told me he would be lecturing in Elmsdale and that I should come meet him. I decided to take Jennifer and go to Elmsdale that week-end.

A couple of months earlier I had applied to a college program, located in Elmsdale. Also I had a job opportunity there. So even if the seminar wasn't interesting, I could check out the area. I had nothing to lose.

Jennifer and I left early that Saturday morning. But when we arrived in Elmsdale, I had difficulty finding the address where the lecture was held. When we finally found it, we were ten minutes late and the lecture had already started.

Peering through the glass door, I saw the room was filled with people. They appeared to be performing a ceremony. An old-looking Lama sat perched on an ornately-decorated throne six feet above the floor, in the front of the hall. Dressed in full regalia, he wore dark crimson robes with an awesome hat that looked like a crown. His eyes were closed.

The sight would scare anyone raised in this culture. Yet it was profoundly compelling. I stood there for a moment not knowing what to do. Then deciding it was too much for me, I began to turn away. Relieved that the lecture had already started, it gave me the excuse I needed to walk away.

Suddenly I noticed a small Asian man in his late fifties. Also dressed in crimson robes, he stood up on the far side of the room. He had been watching us. Stepping through the crowded hall over people, he walked toward the door, toward us. Then he signaled me to enter. At first I looked around, thinking he must mean someone else. He acted as if he knew me. But no one else was there. Finally it dawned on me that he was motioning to us. He was fiercely persistent. Confused, Jennifer and I followed his cues.

I opened the door quietly and entered the room. We stood there for a moment, unable to move through all the people. The man in crimson robes stood five feet away, in front of us. Without saying a word, he impatiently motioned again, for us to follow.

Jennifer and I made our way through the crowd of people and when we arrived at the place he wanted us seated, he forced those already there to move. Respectfully, we followed him. As we sat, I nodded to him in appreciation. He did not respond. I wondered what I was doing!

When I looked up, we were sitting directly below the Lama on the throne. He continued chanting. As I looked up into his eyes, they opened just slightly, as if to acknowledge our arrival, then they closed.

Before I could even get settled, a bolt of lightening cracked through the surrounding atmosphere without a sound and struck the top of my head. My eyes shut. Splitting me in half, a brilliant shaft of iridescent blue-white light plunged into me. Merging into the center of my head, it moved through me with a fathomless intensity. Quietly, Jennifer sat in my lap. Enraptured, my mind *saw* that the shaft of blue-white, radiant light flowed into the Lama. Then moving through his head, it poured into me. The source of this *ray of light* came from above him.

Now I realized it was the same blue-white radiant light coming from my *friends.* It was the same blue-white light that now burns inside of me.

After the ceremony, the Lama seated on the throne whispered something in the ear of one Lama in attendance. He came over to me and invited me to Berkeley, California to attend a week-long teaching. There was little conversation after the ceremony. But Jennifer and I were invited to stay for as long as we liked. Instead I found us a place to eat dinner and drove back to Eugene that night.

I did go to Berkeley, and at the end of May Jennifer and I moved to Elmsdale. The Lama seated on the throne became my teacher. And under his instruction, Jennifer and I lived with and became students of the Asian man in crimson robes who had seated us before him. He was a

Tibetan Lama.

Over the next two years, my daughter and I lived and traveled with a Tibetan Lama we called Rinpoche. (Rinpoche means Precious One. It is a term of endearment and respect, for highly accomplished Tibetan Lamas.) He and his translator became our constant companions. Rinpoche taught, loved, and cared for Jennifer and I, and we loved him.

The lifestyle we lived with Rinpoche was wondrous. But in the spring of 1982 I had reached a point in my life where I didn't want a teacher. Although I deeply appreciated the extraordinary knowledge and love that Rinpoche had shared with Jennifer and myself, I felt it was time to go.

In that same year, I met my husband, Mark. After we were married, we moved back to Eugene where I continued my education. Involved with Jennifer's school, Mark, and work, I focused on our life.

Although my life had been deeply touched by all these powerful experiences I knew that I needed to focus on the present. To me that meant mastering the art of living in the phenomenal worlds.

When we moved back to Eugene I got on with my life and rarely discussed my work with the Rishi or the Tibetan Lamas. It wasn't relevant to my life. Unusual phenomena continued to occur, but I paid little attention.

In November of 1990 another poignant incident occurred. One evening we came home from a movie. The house was dark. When we walked up the stairs from the garage, I looked into the family room. Outside the window, I saw flashing lights reflecting off our deck and windows. Walking over to the window, I tried to see where the lights were coming from. There, hovering above the trees, was an object with green, red, and blue lights flashing. Immediately I thought it was a UFO. Excited, I called Mark to come see it.

My eyes were glued to the object. Mesmerized, I watched as it hovered over the trees. A helicopter would have made noise. This didn't make a sound. I turned my head for only a second to tell Mark to hurry. When I turned back, it was gone!

Mark sauntered over to the window and looked out. Excited, I told him what I had seen. He told me it must have been a helicopter. I wasn't convinced. Although it bothered me, I put it out of my mind. I wondered, where did it go so quickly? A helicopter wasn't that fast. It didn't make sense!

The next morning I awoke with a red mark on my abdomen, two inches from my navel. There was a small puncture in my skin, surrounded by a red circle. The red ring looked like it had been fashioned. It circled the area directly around the wound. I thought I'd been bitten by a spider. It was persistently inflamed.

A year later, I was examining it after I got out of the shower. I thought if I pinched it, maybe I could get rid of it. So I began pinching it between my forefinger and thumb. Suddenly a sharp object pierced me. Something with a sharp point was imbedded just beneath the surface of my skin. It was hard, and had a specific shape. First I was surprised, then I became frightened. I'd never experienced anything like it. It continued to burn and was painful to the touch. Later it turned black and blue. But it never completely went away. It occurred to me to go to a doctor, but it seemed too insignificant to bother.

Throughout the years, many of these incidents could be explained away. But the three days out of my life, the missing-time could not. The incident that occurred in Grand Junction had nagged at me for years. I had quit seeing Karin after our last session. Although I appreciated her help, I no longer wanted her support. Instead I decided to call a therapist I had recently met who had some knowledge of the *Alien Abduction* phenomenon.

We met on the morning of June 16, 1993 at his office. He asked a few personal questions, and after he was satisfied, put me into hypnosis. Taking me back to the summer of 1976, he took me to the moments my daughter and I lay on my bed.

It was around noon and I was feeling nauseous. So I lay down with Jennifer while she took her nap. After she fell asleep, I closed my eyes and saw four *Beings* in the room, two moved toward Jennifer, and the others toward me. Together we were floated in a shaft of light onto a small ship, just above our townhouse. When we entered the ship, we were immediately taken into the examining area. From that point on, I didn't see Jennifer. But I knew she was safe.

The next thing I remembered was standing on the ground, but it wasn't on Earth. The terrain was red clay, with a desert appearance. There was no vegetation. Magnificent jagged red rocks and high plateaus jutted out into a clear, blue sky. Although I didn't see anyone around me, I wasn't alone.

Looking around, I noticed an opening in the huge rock formation on my left. I entered. There, inside the monumental stone was a cavern. At a large rectangular table, sat six golden *Beings* of light. Directly across from each light *Being* was another life form. My usual position was open for me at the end. As I sat across from one of the light *Beings*, an exchange began to occur. Suddenly I realized I too was a golden *Being* of light, with the ability to move through matter. I could transform myself into anything I liked.

Instantly, I saw myself outside the chamber, hovering above the awesome red land formations. Then I began to fly like a bird, soaring through the air. Moving 100 feet above the landscape, I absorbed the scene. Picking up speed, I glided through the canyons and over the towering plateaus with a free abandon. Flying over the surface of the planet, I went faster and faster. Gliding over the tops of the monumental craggy, red rocks, I flew with precision.

As my speed increased, so did my height. I *saw* the planet more clearly. Moving farther and farther away from its surface, something began to happen. The planet a living being was making itself known to me. She was fusing into my soul.

Slowly, bit by bit, my golden particles converged into the red rock formations, the towering hills, and the deep canyons. A warm love surrounded me, embracing my soul. Its dazzling essence fused into me. I *remembered* that we were *One*. Wrapped in her tenderness, and cradled in her wisdom, I bathed in the light of her generous warmth. This planet was where I was from.

CHAPTER TEN:

MORRO BAY

*"To the illumined mind the whole world burns
and sparkles with light."*
Emerson, Journals, 1831.

In July of 1993, Mark and I drove down the California coastline to meet with our dear friends Jeff and Mara, and their two daughters. They had recently bought the home of their dreams at Morro Bay, California. An executive to a large corporation, Jeff had been working abroad since the fall of 1992. Mara was busy flying back and forth from Europe to their home in Southern California, trying to maintain two households. Their daughters Kimberly and Katherine were attending school in the States. It had been too long since our last visit.

Mark and I had known the girls since they were young. We had watched them grow into stunning young ladies. Kimberly, twenty-one, was beautiful, tall, and blonde. Once you penetrated her protective barriers, she willingly shared her marvelous sense of humor. Their youngest daughter, Katherine, also lovely, tall and blonde, was fifteen. She demanded that everyone know what she was thinking. Still, she couldn't hide that twinkle of sweetness showing through her eyes as she defiantly expressed her opinions. It was good to see them.

Mara was a good friend, and winding along the highway, I wondered whether I'd tell her about my encounters. She was beautiful, smart, and had a great sense of humor. Her quick wit and kind, but biting manner were honest and liberating. From the moment we met in 1982, I felt comfortable with her. She was one of those rare people I could tell anything. She wouldn't judge or lecture me. But this, my *dream,* was different.

Breaking through the hills above Morro Bay, we looked down over the small seaside village. Suspended out over the bay was a blanket of silver-gray fog. The weather quickly went from hot and dry, to cool and misty. The change was refreshing.

As we entered the town, we began looking for the street signs to their house. Morro Bay had grown since our last visit. But really there were few changes. The town had retained its charming ambiance. Attractive gift shops and gourmet restaurants lined its brick streets and sidewalks. We found their house, outside town, perched high on a cliff, overlooking the Pacific Ocean.

Awaiting our arrival, Mara and Jeff saw us drive up. They ran to greet us with hugs and kisses. Mark and I were awed by the sweeping views and their magnificent house. Jeff grabbed our bags, leading us into his new showcase. We followed him through the huge double doors as he proudly led us to a beautifully appointed room. Overlooking the ocean, it had staggering views.

After putting our bags away, we walked into the dinning room. Dinner was on the table. As we ate our dinner we all talked at once, as fast as we could, to catch up on all the events happening in our lives. Mark and I were tired from the long drive. So shortly after dinner, we excused ourselves and went to bed.

It was great to see Mara. Her personality was so similar to mine, she felt like part of me. Our husbands continue to share similar interests, making it pleasant for all of us to be together. Kimberly and Katherine were even more beautiful than I remembered.

The following morning I awoke, alone. I assumed Mark and Jeff were off having breakfast. The house was silent. Mark had opened a window during the night and a cool sea-breeze drifted, softly around my head. I heard the waves rolling in off the ocean, lapping up against the rocks at the bottom of the cliff.

When I fully awakened, I rolled out of bed, grabbing my robe. Putting it on, I walked over to the window and looked out over the cliffs, onto the seascape. I gazed down a hauntingly, picturesque beach. Silver-gray and white clouds floated above the water, along the coastline. Shimmering rays of sunlight streamed through small breaks in the clouds. The light sparkled out on the ocean, touching the tips of each wave.

Crawling back into bed, I sat up to meditate. Closing my eyes, I felt *something* calling me. A tingling sensation flooded my body. My *friends* began tugging at my fading consciousness. *They* were out there. Permeating my senses with sweetness, their impressions filled my mind. Their sweet songs echoed, lilting on the breeze, commanding my attention. My body longed to fall into a deep sleep, but my consciousness yearned to be with them, in that place where we are free, where we are *One*.

Experiencing a profound bond to all that was out there, my mind wanted to understand. My consciousness streamed through layers of creation, into other dimensions.

As my minds need to understand gradually slipped away, I saw a circular, metallic ship on the floor of the bay, two-hundred feet off the shoreline. Off in the distance, the sounds of the ocean and the smell of the sea spiraled through my senses.

Instantly I was inside the ship, under the water, at the bottom of the bay. Large, curved windows revealed the ocean floor with all its sea life. Twelve dolphins playfully swam around the ship. For a moment, I watched them in awe! Staring deeply into their eyes, I felt their love. They accompanied the ship. They frolicked in the water, circling the ship, ecstatic to be with their *friends*.

Led into the examining room, my body was checked for physical maladies. But that was not the purpose for this meeting. When the examination was completed, I was escorted into another room and seated in what looked like a dentist's chair. A shiny, metal cylinder came down from the ceiling, above my head. Positioned back at an angle, my head was held in place by two large, gripping pillow-like pads. The cylinder moved down toward my face, and a needle slowly emerged from its center. Piercing through the inside corner of my left eye, it advanced into me. A crystal-like object was attached to the tip of the needle, and implanted in my brain.

When the crystal-like object was placed in position, my head ignited. Immersed in a stunning brilliance, my mind turned into a diamond-like form, illuminating a multi-faceted, crystal-like light. Inside my mind I *saw* sheer sides of a perfectly cut diamond, refracting aspects of light. A blue-white, resplendent light emerged from its center. Emanating out into the atmosphere, it simultaneously drew light in, bringing in the energy from creation.

The next thing I remember, is waking in my bed. A

sense of peace and joy greeted my awakening. Contented, I dressed and went out into the living room.

As I opened my door, a scent of freshly-brewed coffee drifted around me. Confused about the layout of the house, I walked down a hall toward the aroma. I assumed it would lead me to the kitchen, and it did. There was no one there. I wondered where everyone was, yet I was too content to care.

The kitchen overlooked a large living room with vaulted ceilings and expansive windows, facing out onto the ocean and along the beach. Pleased that someone had made some coffee, I poured myself a cup and sat in the living room.

I gazed out over the ocean in silence, sipping my coffee. Drawn into the stillness of an expansive sky, meeting an endless sea with scintillating light moving in and out of me, I was enraptured. Unable to move, I sat listening to the sea gently pounding the shore.

Katherine suddenly danced into the room, touting the arrival of her and her mother. They began telling me that earlier that morning they had spotted ten or twelve dolphins out in the bay. Mara told me it was highly unusual for dolphins to swim into the harbor. Jeff and Mark arrived. They too had seen the dolphins and wondered why they had come into the harbor.

Throughout the years I had heard stories about dolphins helping man in tough situations at sea. I'd heard they displayed joyful and playful natures; that their brains were as developed, or possibly even more developed than human's. Since my *friends* had made themselves known to me, I knew that dolphins were intrinsically connected to them.

I remembered our trip to Las Vegas in February

of 1993. Mark and I had stayed at the Mirage Hotel. Researchers, with the financial aid of the Mirage Hotel, had established a dolphin reserve in order to study their behavior. Mark and I toured the facility.

We walked down into the viewing area, under the water, where windows provided a display of the dolphins. A huge, older male dolphin came close to the window as we approached the glass. He looked directly into my eyes. For a moment, I was surprised. I stopped. Without moving, I stared back. Then he circled back out into the pool, keeping his eyes on me. He passed in front of me, before the window again, examining me with his body, his eyes and his mind. Repeating this behavior, he executed several passes. With each pass I became more aware I was being drawn into him! He *knew* my affiliation with *our friends.*

Telepathically he conveyed his purpose, who he was. His mind was linked with our *friends.* He lived in this dimension, aware of his *Oneness* with all creation. While we were at different levels of *remembering,* he was just like me.

Performing happily, he delighted in our communion. Aware his consciousness was not defined by his body or surroundings, he was filled with joy and peace. Otherwise, the confining environment of those tanks would have devastated him.

Catapulted back into the moment, Mara was asking me how I wanted to spend the day. It was almost time for lunch, so we decided to go into town.

The streets and cafes were crowded with tourists. Fortunately, we found a parking spot across from an interesting-looking restaurant. Mara and I chatted away as we got out of the car and crossed the street.

When I stepped up onto the curb, I saw a man in front of me, sitting in a wheel chair. His back was pushed up against a brick building with a bronze tinted, picture window. He wore a dark green rumpled suit jacket with frayed collar and sleeves. Under his jacket was a dirty white T-shirt. His pants were khaki cotton. The pant legs dangled empty, down to the ground. He'd lost both legs at the knee. His short cropped hair showed portions of his scalp. An unshaven face and ruddy complexion accentuated his clever, piercing blue eyes. While staring into my eyes, he extended his arm. He was holding a tarnished tin cup. Then bracing his wheel chair with the other hand, he looked pathetically into my eyes, begging for money.

As my eyes gazed into his, I *saw* beyond his form. Smiling into his heart with a feeling of euphoria, I experienced the absolute pure love of him. *Seeing* directly into his unique expression, I *saw* he wasn't cripple.

After lunch we spent the afternoon going through small gift shops and enjoying each other's company. Later that evening, when everyone had gone to bed, Mara and I had a chance to talk alone.

Mara mixed her infamous, lethal Margaritas, and we sat in front of a small fire, sipping our drinks and talking in whispers. The sounds of the ocean provided a soothing background. The expansive windows unveiled a stunning horizon. One dark line separated the sea from the sky. Light from the moon filtered through the clouds, glistening on the water. I shared my *dream* with my dear friend.

Mara listened respectfully as I told her my story. I told her about my experiences on that immense ship, located on the Eastern slope of Mt. Rainier when I was three years old. My voice began to transform. My visual perceptions began to alter. I moved directly into that place inside me, where universal consciousness is in control. Mara noticed the change in my voice. She was the first person to ever recognize it. Although I was aware that it had happened many times before.

With my *friends,* I felt a *Oneness.* There was no need for fear. But living in this dimension, sometimes tinges of fear crept into me. I told Mara that the most challenging aspect of these rendezvous with my *friends* were the surgeries.

Mara told me she had no problem with anything I was telling her. She accepted it completely. Her eyes expressed no fear. I wondered whether she would feel so confident if it were happening to her. Quite innocently, she made a mocking comment about people who think their bodies are temples. That was it!

At first, I tried to ignore the implications of her comment. Part of me didn't want to admit she was right. But it all made sense. Sitting there for a moment, I said nothing. Mara had hit it on the head. I *believed* my body *was* a temple. Mara went on talking without realizing her impact on me. Then she noticed my demeanor and stopped. Looking into my eyes she said, "You do! You think your body's a temple." She started laughing at me. She was right!

I hadn't realized myself, until that moment, how attached I was to my *belief.* All those years of religious and cultural training clung to me. Yes, my body is a temple. But not in the way I perceived. My perception had tricked me, keeping me from wholly accepting my relationship with my *friends* and my role in this dimension. Another veil dropped.

The physical procedures accomplished on my body were merely adjustments. Their purpose was to transform my structure. My body was no more than an instrument, a vehicle, a tool to be used in this dimension, in this world. Those modifications enabled my form to sustain higher frequencies of light. Sustaining higher frequencies of light is my purpose.

CHAPTER ELEVEN:

PRECIOUS STONES OF LIGHT

> *"Not by constraint or severity shall you have access to true wisdom, but by abandonment, and childlike mirthfulness. If you would know aught, be gay before it."*
> *Thoreau, Journal*
> *June 23, 1840.*

   Throughout my life I had learned from religion and culture that it was important to get along with others, to meet their needs.   Actively loving myself, I *saw* that my life was a gift. The most powerful offering I could give to creation was to honor and love myself in every way, on every level.

It's easy to say that loving yourself confers the ability to love others. Yet when I took steps to do the things that were right for me, I was often ridiculed by friends and family. Yet those were the steps that brought me to the door of heaven. Loving myself brought me home. Listening to my inner self and acting on those feelings, I served creation throughout my life, without even knowing it.

In September of 1993, I visited some people in San Francisco who had similar experiences with my *friends*. One woman in the group commented on how similar my experiences were to the *Near Death Experience.*

There was no doubt in my mind that I had died to the physical world. Aware that my experiences were joyful and beautiful, I was certain there were others, just like myself, who experienced a profound and awe-inspiring relationship with these *Beings*.

Later that evening, back in my hotel, a vision arose. Overpowered by a swirling sensation of blue-white light, I was forced to sit. Sitting on my bed with my eyes closed, I saw myself standing on a cliff, over looking the ocean. It was a warm summer day, and a soft breeze fluttered across my face. As I looked out over the ocean, I realized I was on a path. Looking down the coastline, I saw the rugged edges of land, eroded away by eons of pounding waves.

Craggy, wind swept trees and shrubs lined the trail. Directly in front of me was a gray metal railing that divided the path from sheer cliffs, dropping down to the sea, about a hundred feet. Jagged cliffs plunged into the ocean. A pale blue sky was fragmented by soft, billowy-white clouds moving across the horizon. The bright golden sun, shown down on the seascape.

Looking down the path, I saw that it wound along the ridge of the cliff. Now walking around a curve, I realized the path took off toward a forest. Before me loomed a huge, black wrought iron fence. Two arched, twenty foot, black wrought iron gates were sustained by massive stone pillars. Ivy leaf designs ornamented the gates, winding through the wrought iron bars. The gates opened. A road suddenly appeared, where the path had been.

In a shimmering flood of silver light appeared a huge,

spherical ship. With no sound, it hovered no more than ten feet above the ground. Surveying its outer surface, I looked for an entrance. Confused, I saw no way in. There were no windows or doors. It hung quiet, in the air. Suspended in the atmosphere, it waited for me to enter. In a flash I found myself inside.

The sphere was composed of the same metallic-like substance that I had seen in the other ships. Yet I was aware that this sphere was somehow different. Standing there in a rounded room, I was alone. As I looked around, I saw controls protruding from the smooth surface. Feeling a sudden pull from my mid-section, a doorway appeared before me. It opened and I entered. Once inside the round room my gaze was drawn to the left, toward an immense, round silver container. The receptacle was bulging with a mound of dazzling jewels. There were thousands of stones in all shapes, sizes, and colors.

Instantly I knew that each stone possessed information. All I had to do was just hold a stone in my hand and knowledge would release itself into me. Each stone housed an aspect of truth about creation. I *remembered* being there before.

One stone seemed to call out to me, asking me to pick it up. It radiated a pulsating luminescent white light. An inch in diameter it appeared as a clear white crystal. As I touched it, another doorway opened, revealing a long dark tunnel. At the end of the tunnel was a brilliant white light. A silhouette of a man stood at the end of the tunnel, defined by the light. It was my *friend*, the *doctor*.

Feelings of great joy and love flooded into me. He told me that it wasn't my time to pass through the door. But he wanted me to know that *they* were part of the *Death Experience*.

My *friends* are the custodians and guardians of this world. They stand at the portals guiding us through each dimension, creating the images we find comforting. Opening our hearts, they lead us home.

In an instant I stood outside the sphere. It hovered in a mist and suddenly I realized that I was at my house in Oregon.

Before the instant I was told, *"It's time to remember,"* I had a *belief.* But the cognition of *Union* was not within my ability to think. *Union* is a **fusion** between the individual self and creation. In one moment, all the particles throughout time and space that made me who I am *converged.* There was no separation between the individual person, Joy, and creation. There was only *One.*

All the pain and joy I had ever experienced was wiped away. While I didn't forget my life experiences, they were overshadowed by the transcendent fabric of luminosity and perfection, underlying all creation. Any remnant left from any failures I might have experienced throughout my life, were simply gone. It was all an illusion. There was never a moment that I wasn't totally living in the pure love of creation. There was never a moment I wasn't totally *Enlightened.*

Belief is a concept of change. Whatever is perceived in this moment, will change the next. The only real security in life is merging into the *Oneness,* fusing back into creation. Accomplishing that *Union,* I transcended the phenomenal worlds of good and evil, right and wrong. Now having come to that place, deep within me, I *saw* that I had always been there, *free.*

The intellect is an excellent tool for living in the phenomenal worlds, but it fails to accommodate *realization.* My *Union* with creation was not something that could be understood with my mind. Yet my intellect, realizing it's finite nature, struggled to survive. It tried to define my new world. Attempting to define the indefinable, it ascribed attributes to that which is beyond thought.

My relationship to the phenomenal worlds, the worlds I see with my eyes, now appears infinitesimal. It does not compare to the vastly infinite creation I experience through my whole being.

My *friends* activated the knowledge, living deep within me. All of us possess all wisdom. It is only choosing to live in that knowledge that determines the separation between those who do, and those who do not.

The encounters with my *friends* ravaged my perception, allowing me to see the truth. My awareness moved from one level of consciousness into new realms, new frontiers of understanding. As my fear gave way, I *saw* through the boundaries of my perception. I *now see* the pure flow of creation moving through everything.

All creation stands by waiting for each of us to *remember* who we are. Loving and nurturing us, she reaches out with her guidance, wisdom and knowledge. Creation flourishes as each of us fulfills our human potential. This is her greatest joy. This is our true purpose, to live in the *One.*

Now *living* in all the layers of creation, I understand the true meaning of prayer. Like a mother with her child, creation longs to make us happy, to fulfill our dreams. She waits in the wings of our drama, yearning to fill our hearts with joy. Knowing every thought, every feeling, at every moment, creation's love for every aspect of her world, good or bad, is fathomless. Longing to answer all our prayers, she sits patiently at our side, waiting for us to ask!

My *friends* had shown me, directly through my life

that if someone in their heart truly seeks the truth, it is revealed.

In one poignant communion, my *friends* told me that I found them beautiful. At first I didn't understand what *they* were saying. Then, I felt them mirroring my minds images back into me. *They saw* more clearly into my soul than I. *They saw* into my heart.

I was profoundly awed by their unique and graceful beauty. When I looked at them, what I saw didn't look like anything I remembered seeing. Yet, I found them enchanting. I saw the light swirling and flowing within them. It was the light of God.

Seeing my feelings before me, I was now aware. My *friends* had lovingly reflected the same intensity of love, appreciation, and beauty back into me that I felt toward them. This was a powerful awakening. *Seeing* their awesome beauty through my heart, I experienced a benevolence, a love, and a feeling of being cherished. The love of all creation was flowing through their form into me.

My *friend's* ability to *see* within me, revealed how transparent we all are. There is nothing we can hide. Through them, I *saw* that I did the same with others. *Seeing* into other's worlds, I watch creation use my form to draw their feelings to the surface, into their awareness. In visions and mental images, my *seeing* is often in stunning detail.

The relationship I share with my *friends,* takes place on another level. It is not linear. They are interdimensional. Our ever-present communion flows into me from finer levels of creation, where the power is limitless, where this world is upheld. It is from these subtler layers of creation the material worlds are sustained.

Liquid light streams into me, with an intense

knowledge that saturates my cells. It is not limited by thought or word. Immersed in love, creation uses my form to translate information. Transmitting knowledge from finer and more powerful levels of creation, I bring that light into this world.

What is imposed into my mind isn't totally adaptable to human language. Its vastness cannot be defined by our human parameters, in time or space. But within a touch, a glance, a smile, and the very sound of my voice, creation flows out touching all those around me, and without them even knowing, awakens their soul. It no longer matters what I say or do. Everything that flows through me exists to serve all creation.

With no attachment to the phenomenal worlds, or to the feelings that pass through me, I have no longing. I am home. Joy was born to merge back into creation. Once that merging occurred, I *saw* myself as pure light, without form.

When the light of the soul is ignited, darkness is dispelled. Like when a light is turned on in a dark room there is no fear because you can see clearly all that is in the room. There is no right or wrong, good or evil. I see the world of duality as two sides of the same coin.

In my quiet moments, my *friends come to me.* I feel their sweet cool breath, wafting across my body. Tenderly caressing my face, *they* gently blow their soft, sweet breath into my mouth. Ever so sweetly I feel them kissing me, loving me, as *they* breathe the breath of life into my form. Passing through my body, their blue-white, crystal light drenches each atom, ever-deepening our love, bringing me to the essence of creation. *It is here that I am, and know all things.*

Having the ability to move through all the layers of creation, many perceive my *friends* at different levels, in different ways, as different things. Often *they* are perceived as supernatural. Yet their ability to manipulate matter comes to them from their level of service. The task my *friends* fulfill, is the facilitation of greater awareness. *They* assist and sustain the flow of an ever-expanding universe. *They have always been here.* Serving as guides through inner dimensions, *they* have led me ever further into myself. Never presenting themselves as the truth, or the creator, their love has guided me home, back to the core of creation.

Now I *remember* who I am. Through that *remembering* I fulfill my human potential, living in the light. *Realizing* and *acknowledging* my part in creation, I experience the whole.

Constantly amazed at the exquisite synchronisity in which our lives are intertwined, I *see* that everything is absolutely perfect. Memories come into me, both from the future and the past. Through the flow of life, creation speaks to me, sharing her sweet secrets. I experience infinite joy. Every moment I live is in the *Oneness.* I am, and at the same time flow in the river that is life. I'm aware of my place in the world of perfection and beauty. Always feeling my *Oneness* with the universe, I'm swept along like a river, yet standing in perfect harmony upon the bank, watching.

Becoming *One* with the Earth's wealth and knowledge, I became *One* with all things. *Seeing* the interconnected role we each play, I deeply understand the richness of the American Indians, Hindus, and Tibetan traditions. Their traditions have teachings that discuss the role of *Beings* from other dimensions, participating in our lives. They never lost contact with the Earth. Revering and respecting her, they knew their souls served creation, as each aspect of creation serves the whole.

The days that someone could affect my mood, or how I perceived myself, are over. An inner confidence, a sense of self-sufficiency, and a knowing of who I am, lingers always, deep within me. Now an incident that previously might have caused me suffering, has no hold. I experience the feelings of life as a current, a flow, passing through me. One minute they're here! The next they're gone! My emotion is diminished. Yet the feelings I experience are far more profound.

I live out my blueprint, aligned with the will of creation, totally aware of my relationship to all things and my own synchronisity. Every action, thought, and behavior comes to fulfill my role in creation's design. There is nothing that we, as separate individuals, can do to change the course of life. We cannot stop the river from rushing to the sea. Nature will always prevail.

Each of us is made from particles of creation. We are all the same substance. We are all connected by our very nature. It is in that place *we all have the ability to see into other realms.* It is in that place I am conscious of being connected to my *friends.* Our minds function on the same frequencies, like a radio.

Sensing everything I experience and feel, within moments my *friends* respond to all my needs. Joy and laughter are my constant companions even when to others I may appear angry.

Now operating in the world from a place deep within me, I neither judge, nor praise. I live in the experience of joy and bliss, the transcendent. The energy of creation from which all things flow, is ever-felt within me. Lying at my core, speaking to me sweetly, is the still and peaceful waters of my soul.

In the beginning of this flowing awareness, my *friends* told me to call a woman whom I didn't really know. I had met her once or twice and had no real affiliation with her. Yet I could feel them pressing me to call her. *They* wanted me to tell her something. Yet I thought to myself, how bizarre. I don't want to call someone that I don't even know and tell her, "Wait for the light, and do not be afraid when it comes for you." It seemed to have no meaning.

The feelings persisted until finally one morning I picked up the phone and dialed her number. When she answered the phone, her voice exposed a flat affect. The inflection was typically depressive. After our salutations, I told her that I didn't understand why I was calling, but I had the feeling to call and share some thoughts with her. Without referring to where these impressions had come from, I began to tell her what my *friends* had told me to say, exactly as they had said it. Instantly she began sobbing. Her husband had died a year ago that day. She had been sitting there contemplating suicide.

She was not the last person I was led to who was contemplating suicide. I am guided to be with the people I need to be with, in each moment.

For those whose time has come to *remember*, nothing can stop their *remembering*. For those whose time has not yet arrived, there is nothing they can do to make it happen. But no one is forgotten. For those who do not yet *remember*, the seeds have been planted for another time, in the time-space continuum. There is no hurry. There are no winners or losers. Everything is unfolding exactly as it should. Every action in the universe is part of the whole design.

My *friends* showed me that this planet is going through a transformation. While it may *appear* to come in loss of life, alteration of continents, floods, collapse of governments and economies, negative weather conditions, volcanic eruptions and earth quakes, this is the normal and necessary process of expansion and growth. *They* told me that there would be thousands of people dying to this world in single moments. Two weeks later the earthquake in India was reported on the news. Thousands of people died that night.

Our perceptions of form keep us from *seeing* the beauty of the life process. All of life is change. All living things in physical form are constantly changing. In that change, the process of being born and dying is perfect. The important thing to remember when a loved one dies, is that there is no death. There is only change! They are not leaving us, or going anywhere. There is no where to go!

It is easy to be unhappy and to find reasons to suffer in a world that is full of sorrow and loss. It takes true courage to find love, feel love, and sustain it, to live your life in true joy and not allow the phenomenal worlds of positive and negative pull you in.

My most cherished task is to remain blissful, amid the constant, increasingly negativity of this world. Real inner joy, not contrived, in and of itself, is a powerful act and a great benefit to all life.

CHAPTER TWELVE:

THEIR MESSAGE TO US IN THEIR WORDS

*"There is no purifier, like knowledge in
this world:
time makes man find himself in his heart.
Bhagavadgita, 4, tr. P. Lal.*

"The light will first emerge silently in the souls of men and woman around the world. Then will come the quiet brilliance that emerges in the brain and extends out, reaching the farthest corners of this universe and on into the next universe.

There is a quiet call to awaken the sleeping souls who walk in the dream-state on this planet. That call is now being answered. Many have come to share and watch this beautiful planet being born into a new form. There is much joy and happiness at this awakening.

We have come to help in the birth process. In this new awakening is the loss of other aspects of the entity which are no longer needed. It is in this transition that we serve the beings of this planet.

Many of you do not as yet understand what is happening to your planet. You perceive that it is dying. But you do not see the incredible beauty and life emerging. Yes, the planet appears to be suffering, and air quality appears to be dismal and non-nurturing. But out of this suffering will emerge a new planet-being full of light and brilliance, in complete alignment with creation.

Creation has watched this planet moving into this process for sometime with great joy and pleasure. This is the self of the creator experiencing itself in all its splendor and diversity. You can make this process difficult for yourselves and it will occur. Or you can enjoy and watch the process and it will occur. The choice is yours. Energy is Energy. It is your choice as to how you choose to perceive it. We are here to tell you that you can enjoy every minute of your life, during the great shift now occurring.

Feel everything. Do not let anyone tell you how to think or feel. The answers for your life come from inside your physical form, from the soul that is housed inside your body. It can speak to you and tell you where you need to go and what you need to do, at each given moment.

Do not be fooled by those who wish to control your belief. Do not hold tight to any belief. Allow it all to pass through you. Belief is merely thought, and thought is part of the world of change. There is only one part of your being, the bigger part, which knows there is nothing here but love, peace, and joy. It is that part you must be based in.

Allow all the experiences that come to you, pass through you like the wind passes through the trees. Allow yourself to enjoy the wind and feel it soothe your face and merge through your physical body. But know that it is not permanent. And while it is not you, it is the experience of life that you have chosen. So cherish and relish it. But let it go.

Each experience that you have in your life brings to you an aspect of yourself. Good or bad, it is all the same creation. It is the dance of life. Flowing like the river into the ocean of love and kindness, all One.

Each expression only manifests to experience itself and then move on to the next experience. You are in this world, but you are not of it. You only manifest yourself in creation in order to experience yourself, and if you remembered who you are, you wouldn't experience the feelings of separation. Then you could never know the human experience and the joy of uniting once again with creation. It is all absolute perfection.

There is nothing in the universe, no act, no thought, no dream, no wish that goes unnoticed. It is all honored and cherished. Everything you see, everything you hear, everything you taste, touch and smell, is all part of your experience. It is the diversity that creates the joy in each experience. The diversity creates a fuller experience of the *One*.

Loneliness is a feeling of separation from yourself and cannot be fulfilled another way, than through your soul, your Creator. In spiritual terms, you must open yourself to God from within. Then all those things in life you thought were so difficult, become easy. When you open up to the fullness and beauty of life, it opens itself to you. As you serve life, it serves you. As your heart opens and serves God within, all things become available. There is no pain.

As the light of God flows into this planet, you can either allow it in, or inhibit it. There is little choice. It will occur. The light shines down on all equally. Only *you* have forgotten who you are, and what you are doing here. Belief in the *unknown* is your only security. Knowing that all things will be fulfilled, and all dreams met, is hard to imagine when your only reality is the phenomenal worlds. Go within, and all your dreams will come true, all of them. It is all here for you to enjoy. It is all here for you to have. Be as a child in the world, and know that all your dreams will be answered.

Loss and suffering are part of this dimension. No one is exempt from the experience. It is part of life. You cannot hide from pain. You have to go through it. However pain is only one dimensional. You are all multidimensional beings.

Peace will be the main process of development among the people who will inhabit the earth in the New Age. Many have been called to serve during this transition and feel the joy in being part of the new growth now emerging. It is for this reason we are making ourselves known, to share knowledge with you at this time."

ABOUT THE AUTHOR

Joy S. Gilbert was born in Seattle, Washington. Raised in Seattle's rich multi-cultural environment, she developed an intense interest in human behavior. Her inquisitive nature led her abroad during the late 1960's, where she lived in India with a Rishi. Later during that time she traveled through Europe while living in Italy. Returning home from her first trip to Europe in 1972, Joy lectured, taught meditation, and conducted seminars and retreats throughout the United States. In 1974 she went back to Europe and lived in Brunnen, Switzerland on Lake Lucerne.

In 1979 under unusual circumstances Joy became a student and friend of a Tibetan Lama. She and her daughter lived and traveled with he and his translator until 1982.

Holding a Certificate in Early Childhood Education and a BS in Psychology from the University of Oregon, Joy graduated Summa Cum Laude, Phi Beta Kappa. There she also received the Mortar Board Award for high scholastic achievement and belonged to the Golden Key Honors Society. Participating in Graduate Studies in Neuroscience and Counseling she worked in the field of early childhood education, and later as a Program Director for a local child abuse agency. Joy has been married since 1982 and is the mother of a daughter in college. Presently she is the vice-president of a successful retail business in Eugene, Oregon.

177

Coming to grips with the shattering nature of an *Alien Abduction*, in Sisters, Oregon on January 31st, 1993, Joy successfully integrated this phenomenon into her life. Although her experience, like others, was initially one of terror, she opened herself to its gifts. Joy was transformed. She is forever changed and deeply touched by these extraordinary and loving *Beings* who she now calls her *friends*.

Unlike many who discuss fearful and negative encounters with *Alien Beings*, *Joy experienced a fusion into them and then into creation. She is never apart from their sweet and loving qualities. They are One.* Impelled by her *friends* to share her story and their message, Joy wrote *It's Time to Remember*.

INDEX

TO ORDER

IT'S TIME TO REMEMBER
A Riveting Story of One Woman's Awakening to Alien Beings
by
Joy S. Gilbert

Telephone Orders: Toll Free 1- 800- 935- 2327 (BEAR)
Have your Mastercard or Visa ready.

For Postal Orders Send your check or money order to:
Laughing Bear Publishing
P. O. Box 40788
Eugene, Oregon 97404
503- 935- 5256
Please fill out the following information and return with
your check or money order. (NO C.O.D.)

Name:_____
Address:_____
City:_____ State:_____
Zip:_____

Phone:(_____)_____
Ck__ Money Order__
Mastercard or Visa #_____
Signature_____ Exp. Date_____

Please Send _____ copies @ $19.95 U.S.A.
$26.96 Canadian
Shipping and Handling: $ 3.00 per book

If you would like further information about the up coming
book, written by this author, please fill out this form, then
send it to the address above. You will receive an
announcement when it is in print.

TO ORDER

IT'S TIME TO REMEMBER
A Riveting Story of One Woman's Awakening to Alien Beings
by
Joy S. Gilbert

Telephone Orders: Toll Free 1- 800- 935- 2327 (BEAR)
Have your Mastercard or Visa ready.

For Postal Orders Send your check or money order to:
Laughing Bear Publishing
P. O. Box 40788
Eugene, Oregon 97404
503- 935- 5256

Please fill out the following information and return with
your check or money order. (NO C.O.D.)

Name: _C O R d N a_

Address: _3 d A B - u n i t_

City: _F R e S n o_   State: _C a l i f o r n i a_

Zip: _1 9 8 0, 1 9 8 1, 1 9 8 7 . . ._

Phone:(_2 5 3_) _8 4 9 - 3 3 4 9_

Ck ✓ Money Order ✓

Mastercard or Visa # _8 5 2 6 9 2_

Signature _Caitlin Quing_   Exp. Date _Dec. 26, 1980_

Please Send _____ copies @ $19.95 U.S.A.

$26.96 Canadian

Shipping and Handling: $ 3.00 per book

If you would like information about the up coming book,
written by this author, please fill out the form, then send it
to the address above. You will receive an announcement
when it is in print.

TO ORDER

IT'S TIME TO REMEMBER
A Riveting Story of One Woman's Awakening to Alien Beings
by
Joy S. Gilbert

Telephone Orders: Toll Free 1- 800- 935- 2327 (BEAR)
Have your Mastercard or Visa ready.

For Postal Orders Send your check or money order to:
Laughing Bear Publishing
P. O. Box 40788
Eugene, Oregon 97404
503- 935- 5256

Please fill out the following information and return with
your check or money order. (NO C.O.D.)

Name: ESTEBAN
Address: 772 E. MARW AVE.
City: Fresno State: California
Zip: _____

Phone: (253) 849-3349
Ck √ Money Order √
Mastercard or Visa # 85 26 92
Signature Esteban Quing Exp. Date Dec. 26. 1980

Please Send _____ 3 _____ copies @ $19.95 U.S.A.
                                       $26.96 Canadian
Shipping and Handling: $ 3.00 per book

If you would like information about the up coming book,
written by this author, please fill out this form, then send it
to the address above. You will receive an announcement
when it is in print.